Big Savings

Small Business, Big Savings

Laura Teller and Warren R. Schatz

HarperPerennial
A Division of HarperCollins Publishers

HarperCollins books may be purchased for educational, business, or sales promotional use. For information, please write: Special Markets Department, HarperCollins Publishers, Inc., 10 East 53rd Street, New York, NY 10022.

FIRST EDITION

Library of Congress Cataloging-in-Publication Data
Teller, Laura, 1956–
    Small business, big savings / Laura Teller & Warren R. Schatz—1st ed.
      p. cm.
    Includes index.
    ISBN 0-06-273298-6
    1. Purchasing—Directories. 2. Office equipment and supplies—Purchasing—Directories. 3. Small business—United States—Management. I. Schatz, Warren R., 1945– . II. Title.
HF5437.T45   1995
338.4'0029'6—dc20   94-25568

95 96 97 98 99 CC/HC 10 9 8 7 6 5 4 3 2 1

Contents

Introduction

We wrote this book because we needed it ourselves.

Each of us runs a small business—Warren owns a corporate communications firm and produces records, and Laura is a principal in the marketing and strategy consultancy she cofounded several years ago. And, like all small business owners, our responsibilities extend beyond merely "doing our jobs" to doing *all* jobs: marketing, sales, product development, service, manufacturing—and, of course, purchasing.

That's where the idea for this book came from. Both of us absolutely *hate* to spend more than we need to for supplies and other business-related merchandise—because even though tax-deductibility takes some of the sting out, we're still aware that every purchase leaves us with less money in our pockets at the end of the year.

We come by this penny-pinching honestly. Warren's father used to drive by the warehouses in Brooklyn to see what bargains he could pick up. One time, he came home with 50,000 paper napkins for $10. Another time, he found an unbelieveable deal on paint, bought 10 gallons, and proceeded to redecorate the entire interior of their house. (Trouble was, it was army olive drab—but a bargain's a bargain!) One Christmas, he even bought a new set of tires just to get the free Christmas record.

As for Laura, her parents love garage sales, auctions and flea markets—and delight in finding cheap travel deals. Her mother jokes that she knows the word "sale" in every language. Mom buys dented cans at a discount, sometimes without labels—hoping she's buying tuna fish and not cat food! And talk about never throwing anything out—when Laura was growing up, the family had three TV sets on top of each other. The top one had picture but no sound, the middle one had sound but no picture, and the bottom one didn't work at all—but it was one of the first TVs ever made, and Dad thought he'd eventually make money on it. (He did.)

Genetically, we're both bargain hunters. Unfortunately, we don't have the time to shop around to make sure we're getting the absolute lowest prices. Both of us have (knock wood) thriving businesses that already take up a big chunk of our waking hours. So, sometimes we have just settled for paying more than we know we should, because it's been easier than calling around and hoping we'll be able to find the "magic source" for the lowest price on the particular thing we happen to need.

One day we were sitting around at the local coffee shop, and the subject came up. "Someone must have written something for small businesses on this subject—sort of like a 'purchasing agent in a book,' " one of us said.

"What a great idea!" said the other one. "Let's check it out!" So we paid the check and trundled down to the local bookstore. And there on the small business shelves. . . .

No dice. There were books on marketing, on selling, on financing, on what businesses to buy, on how to manage employees and time—but nothing on where and how we could save money on purchasing the basic goods and services that keep an office running.

At this point, we still couldn't believe no one had done this. So over the next several weeks, we kept looking—seeking out larger bookstores, business specialty bookstores, business school bookstores. No success. We asked around—other friends with small businesses, people who consult to small businesses. To a person, no one had ever seen such a book. But almost to a person, they said they'd happily *buy* such a book if they ever got their hands on it. So one of us found out what goes in a book proposal, and we wrote one and sent it off to a couple of business book publishers.

Many months, three drafts, thousands of phone calls, hundreds of pounds of catalogs and a couple of all-nighters later, here's the book we wanted and couldn't buy. In it, we've included not only great low-cost sources for all sorts of things businesses need, but we've also gathered general tips on how you can save money in that area—like how and what you can negotiate, easy ways to manage your operations to save even more, and many other things that experienced purchasers of these goods and services know. We've put these general tips at the beginning of each chapter, and then placed the low-price sources at the end.

So, here's our suggestion: *Read or skim the text first, then turn to the sources.* That way, you'll get a general overview of the purchasing process and your options in the area before you go charging off to buy.

A couple of other things to bear in mind:

- We checked telephone numbers, names and addresses as close to the printing deadline as we could—but things change. If you have trouble locating a business, try calling the "800" directory first (1-800-555-1212).
- We've determined low-cost sources the same way you'd do it, by getting catalogs from many different suppliers and comparing their prices. When possible, we tried to compare exact equals—e.g., prices on the same brand name products. Where it wasn't possible, we tried to compare products with similar specs. But we also gave the supplier a break if they guaranteed to meet or beat competitors' prices or if they had low-cost "house" brands. We think this method has allowed us to eliminate suppliers who really aren't "discount," and to retain suppliers who meet a certain threshhold of low pricing.
- We used some other selection criteria, as well. Although we can't (and don't) guarantee that you'll never get "burned" by any of the suppliers in this book, we have tried to select suppliers who have been in business for a while, offer good service support, and back up their products and services with money-back guarantees.
- We know there's more out there. You probably have some great sources that we haven't yet discovered. If so, would you do us a favor? Drop us a line, in care of HarperCollins Reference, 10 East 53rd Street, New York, NY 10022, telling us the name, telephone number and product line of the supplier. We'd also like to hear from you if you've had some particularly good or bad experiences with any of the sources we've included here. Please let us know, so we can pass it along to your fellow small business owners and managers. Also let us know if you'd like more or different information in the book. We'll incorporate it into the next edition!

Acknowledgments

If we had known what we were getting into, we'd probably never have embarked on this task. (We're staying out of coffee shops in the future!) But it's turned out to be a great journey. We're so grateful to the following people for their assistance, understanding and support:

Philip Cowan, for his ongoing counsel and perspective—a great lawyer and wonderful friend; Doug Duda, for his generous spirit, love and faith; Michael Gorman, who gave Laura "time off" without ever complaining; Bonnie Hiller, who taught us how to write a book proposal; Dan McNamee, who gave us a foot in the door; Mike Schatzkin, who opened that door even wider; Sandi Kimmel, Eric Schatz, Walter Schatz, Roberta Lawrence and Kadri Kristjuhan, who helped us research various subjects and supplied us with the best in reading material; Christy Lemmon, who checked all the telephone numbers and addresses; Claire Poole, who kept the catalogs under control; and Ken Swezey and Janet Greeberg, who put together a deal everyone could live with. And thanks most of all to our editor, Rob Kaplan, who gave us space, pushed us when we needed it and believed in this project. Thank you, Rob.

This book is dedicated by Laura with love and gratitude to her first and best editors, Oscar and Estelle Teller. Start combing the garage sales for a magnet big enough to keep this on the refrigerator!

This book is dedicated by Warren to the memory of his father, Joseph, who loved a bargain, and to his mother, Rose Moss, who never bought retail.

1

Banking Services and Checks

Maybe it's because they deal in money, but banks seem to have an uncanny way of finding ways to get into your pocket. They slap charges on everything you can think of, and many things you probably *haven't* considered. In New York City, where we're from, basic checking account fees can easily top $300 a year! And, of course, if your business creates a high volume of bank transactions, costs can be far higher.

There is no need to be held hostage to bank fees, however. Remember one thing: With banks, *almost everything is negotiable*. Depending on your balances and your volume of transactions, the bank officer has the right to waive or lower fees and get you special handling or free services. Sometimes, he or she also has a good deal of clout in getting you lower-cost loans or lines of credit. So before you set up an account (or pay one more month's activity fee) sit down with the bank officer and ask what he or she will do to get (or keep) your business. Remember: If one bank isn't flexible, the next one might be. Smaller, hungrier banks are usually the most willing to deal, as are banks that make a practice of catering to "middle market" concerns and small businesses.

You should talk to at least three institutions before making any banking or credit decision. Some of the major areas on which to focus your discussion include:

- *Monthly account fees.* What are they? Are they based on level of activity, are they flat fees or flat fees plus charges for each transaction? What

1

might this add up to for your business? Often, the bank will waive or reduce your fees if you keep a minimum amount in your account. If so, what's the minimum amount, and does the money you have in linked accounts (e.g., a money market or savings account) count toward the total balance?

- *Earnings Credit Rate ("ECR").* Even in a checking account, your corporation's deposits earn credit that can offset some or all of your account fees. (Essentially, the bank pays a form of "interest" on the "average earning balance," i.e., your average collected balance less government-mandated reserves). Check what the bank is paying (the rate varies widely from bank to bank) and what deductions they are taking on your average collected balance (formulas also vary). The easiest way to obtain this information is to ask the bank for your company's "account-analysis statement."

- *Per-transaction fees.* What do they charge you to write a check, get a cashier's check or make a deposit? What do they charge for Electronic Funds Transfer? What is the price premium you'll pay for "unencoded" deposits (e.g., handwritten checks that cannot be scanned) or checks processed through nonlocal Federal Reserve banks? Depending on your business, different types of transaction fees will be paramount, so focus on these.

- *Charges for other services.* Depending on your business, you may need other services: wire transfer, letters of credit, lines of credit or cash management consulting services. Don't forget to compare fees on these services as well.

- *Fees for ATM use.* If you routinely use ATMs for withdrawals or deposits, beware: most banks charge for these services, and fees are rocketing up. In 1993 alone, they increased 38%. Today, many banks charge 40¢ or more per transaction, and some are pushing the $1 mark. If you are a heavy user, compare fees. (You might also wish to limit your dependence on ATMs. Why not actually talk to a live human being when you make your deposit?)

- *Fees to pay your bills.* Automatic draft deduction, for such things as car leases, health insurance and mortgage payments, can save time and ensure that critical bills get paid on time—but it can also be expensive. Moreover, you should never assume that the bank's statement is correct—check it out every month, and if a mistake occurs, take care of it immediately, as it can be a nightmare to try to change once time goes by.

- *Fees for bounced checks.* Let's face it, sometimes you make a mistake—

you're late to the bank with a deposit, or you've added wrong—and your check bounces. Bounced checks are embarrassing enough, without the added pain of a hefty fee. So, compare what different banks charge, try to arrange for an automatic credit line or bounce protection (don't forget to ask what they charge for this!), and, of course, keep a close eye on your accounts so that you don't end up overdrawn. You might also meet with your account officer and arrange with him or her to alert you if you're in danger of becoming overdrawn. (But don't count on this—overdraft fees are a key contributor to a bank's bottom line. According to the *New York Times,* check overdraft fees exceeded $4 billion dollars in 1992—and 84% of this was profit!)

- *Fees for blank checks.* Selling you blank checks is a huge money-maker for banks; if you're still buying them there instead of from the check-printing companies themselves, you're paying double or more what you could be. In the "Sources" section of this chapter, we provide the names of direct-to-you check printers.
- *Length of "hold" time.* When will the bank clear the check you've deposited? Is the "hold" period calculated on calendar days or business days? Hold time has a critical impact on your business, not only in terms of cash flow, but also in earned interest. For instance, did you know that if your bank has a 7-day hold policy, the yield on a 60-day deposit drops by 12%, and the annual yield on an 8% deposit drops almost a full percentage point?

One thing to note: although it's tempting, we urge you not to select a bank solely on the basis of fees. Service can be as just as important. Check for convenience (hours of operation, location); ease of use (short lines, lots of tellers, enough cash machines, express deposit machines); range of services offered (e.g., letters of credit, bank by phone or computer); accessibility of bank officers. You might also want to take into consideration other services focused on small and growing businesses, such as consulting assistance and reduced or waived fee products and services. Don't miss out on:

- *Mortgage programs.* Some banks provide special mortgage programs (e.g., reduced rates, no-points, etc.) for small businesses. This is a great, free benefit for you and your employees. Note that your business may not need to have funds on deposit to qualify for the above programs; some banks are happy to do it solely for the profit they make on mortgages.
- *Free checking for employees.* It's nice to be able to offer this as a perq for

your employees, particularly as it doesn't cost you anything or require any extra administration on your part.

- *Cash management techniques.* Some banks offer one-on-one consulting to help you get the most out of your cash on hand.
- *Free seminars.* Some banks sponsor presentations for small businesses, many of which center on banking and financing. But we've seen some banks offer seminars on a range of other topics of interest to small businesses.

SOURCES:

BANKING SERVICES AND CHECKS

There's no one-stop magical bank that you can access to save money. The best way to obtain the best combination of low bank charges and good service is to shop around in your local area, using the tips we've outlined in the beginning section of this chapter.

Buying blank checks directly, instead of through your bank is a different story. There are a number of central sources that can save you 60% or more off bank prices. *Make sure, however, that the checks meet or exceed the ANSI standards set by the American Bankers Association; all the sources listed here do.*

It's easy to order, but remember that for security purposes, suppliers generally won't accept phone orders on the first order. However, once you've set up an account, most suppliers will accept your reorder by phone or fax.

A final tip: You'll save even more if you buy checks in quantity.

CHECKS IN THE MAIL
P.O. Box 7802
Irwindale, CA 91706

1-800-733-4443

Checks in the Mail has some interesting designs, and also offers a full line of computer checks. You can get 300 checks and 200 deposit slips for under $30—a significant saving when you think that some banks charge $60 or more.

Outlet Type: Catalog house.

Product Line: Broad line of business and consumer checks, including computer checks. Deposit slips, binders.

Fax: 1-818-962-3087

Information: Brochure.

**Orders Accepted
By:**   Mail for first order; thereafter by phone or mail.

Payment: MasterCard or Visa on phone orders, by mail, check or money orders.

Delivery: Normal delivery in 2–3 weeks with $1 shipping/handling charge. Fed Ex 2nd-day available for an additional $5. Gold Start service is available for an additional $12; includes 2-day processing and delivery by 3rd business day.

Guarantees: Work is unconditionally guaranteed. Checks will be reprinted or money refunded.

CURRENT

P.O. Box 18500
Colorado Springs, CO 80935-8500

1-800-533-3973

Current has been in the business of check printing for 10 years, and prides itself on the high quality paper it uses and the fact that its checks surpass American Bankers Association standards for security and printing. It stands behind its work with an unconditional money back guarantee, and offers savings that can exceed 75% off some banks' charges.

Outlet Type: Catalog house.

Product Line: Business and personal checks and deposit tickets, including carbonless duplicate style, in a fairly limited range of colors and styles. Check binders. Although planning to add computer checks, at this writing do not offer them.

Fax: 1-719-548-9571 (Note: Current prefers telephone or mail orders.)

Information: Brochure.

**Orders Accepted
By:**   First order: mail only. Reorders: mail, telephone, or fax.

Payment: First order: check only. Subsequent orders: check, MasterCard, Visa, Discover (two box minimum order size).

Delivery: Regular check delivery takes 2–3 weeks from the time you mail your order. FedEx 2nd day service or priority mail available at extra charge.

Guarantees: Work is unconditionally guaranteed. Checks will be reprinted or money refunded.

DESIGNER CHECKS
920 19th Street N
Birmingham, AL 35202

1-800-239-9222

Designer offers a broad line of designs; although they don't offer the large business-sized checks in a desk-book format, they do have computer checks and three-on-a-page wallet-sized checks. All checks meet American Bankers Association standards.

Outlet Type: Catalog house.

Product Line: Personal checks in many designs (wallet and desk versions); computer checks, leather and fabric checkbook covers.

Fax: 1-205-328-3815

Information: Brochure.

Orders Accepted By: First-time orders accepted only by mail; reorders accepted by telephone.

Payment: Checks on first orders. MasterCard, Visa on reorders.

Delivery: Normal delivery in 2–3 weeks from day the order is received; 90¢ shipping/handling fee. Expedited handling is available at extra charge, and can reduce delivery time to 5–7 days.

Guarantees: Satisfaction guaranteed. Work will be redone or money refunded.

IMAGE CHECKS

P.O. Box 548
Little Rock, AR 72203-0548

1-800-562-8768

Image offers a broad line of business checks, including laser and continuous form. And all designs are the same price—saving you 50% and more off bank charges.

Outlet Type:	Catalog house.
Product Line:	Business checks, including computer (laser and continuous form), personal checks, checking accessories, such as stamps and binders.
Telephone:	1-800-562-8768
Fax:	1-501-225-0429 (Not available for ordering).
Information:	Brochure, phone.
Orders Accepted By:	Mail.
Payment:	Check, cash or money order.
Delivery:	2 weeks for businesses (via UPS). Expedited delivery is available at extra charge.
Guarantees:	Satisfaction guaranteed, or work will be redone or money refunded.
See Also:	Entries in Chapter 13, "Printing, Stationery, Business Forms and Specialty Papers":

- The Business Book
- Deluxe Business Forms and Supplies
- The Drawing Board
- McBee Systems
- Moore Business Products

2

Books and Publications

A business colleague of our was complaining that when she tallied her business's itemized expenses for tax purposes she was shocked to find that her yearly bill for publications, books and magazines and other media-related expenses was about double what she intuitively thought it was going to be. In fact, it topped $1000!

Here's why: Her business pays for two daily newspapers, costing about 50¢ a day. Even with a subscription, the *Wall Street Journal* costs about 50¢ a day, and two people in her office receive it. The business has subscriptions to a couple of trade magazines and newsletters, an investment newsletter, two or three general business magazines and the local business journal. Every once in a while, she has to buy a number of special interest magazines in order to complete a project or pitch new business. As a marketing professional, she has to have cable TV at the office; the basic service tops $200 per year. Once she adds in books and books on tape, it becomes clear why keeping current on business news and trends takes a bite out of her bottom line.

It's easy enough, however, to save on publications and other media-related expenses. Some suggestions:

- *Get a subscription—don't pay newsstand prices.* If you read the publication regularly, getting a subscription will easily save you 50% or more on newspapers and magazines.

- *Make sure you read it and need it.* Periodically, cull your reading list. Cancel subscriptions or stop buying publications that you really don't read or aren't as informative as they should be. You'll have more time *and* more money.
- *Use the library.* Why pay for a book when you can borrow it for free? That goes for videos and books on tape, too. Our rule: Unless it's a reference tool that you're going to use all the time (e.g., this book!), find it at the library.
- *If you commute, check the train's seats.* Many people leave their just-read newspapers behind. If you don't mind "used news" you can get your morning paper for free.
- *Read free when you shuttle.* If you take the air shuttles between New York and Boston or Washington, grab a briefcase full of the free magazines and newspapers made available to passengers.
- *Check rental sources.* Why buy when you can rent at a far lower cost? We've included one nationwide source for business/motivational audio and video tapes (see "Redding" in our listings) but you may be able to find a local source as well.
- *Trade with friends and colleagues.* If you do this, however, be sure to make a list of who has your books, and to whom you owe books. Books have a way of getting lost.
- *Buy one subscription for the office and use routing slips or have a central lending library.* That way, many people get the information for the same cost.
- *Check your professional organization or trade group.* They may have a library of books in your subject area.
- *Wait for the paperback.* Hardcover prices can be up to four or five times the paperback price. Do you really need that hardcover book as soon as it comes out?
- *Don't overlook used bookstores.* One of us has a local bookstore that gives us credit for used books we bring in, and offers enormous discounts on used books. We've built up quite a nice library of business classics that way.
- *Browse the bargain bins of bookstores.* It's a nice thing to do on the weekend, and sometimes you can find gems.
- *Warehouse clubs offer a great new option.* It can really be hit or miss, but warehouse clubs sometimes have incredible values on books and magazines—up to 70% off the cover price.
- *Consider joining a "Business Book Club."* Book clubs offer their mem-

bers just-published books at a significant discount. The hitch is that you're often committed to purchasing a set amount of books in a certain time frame, and you have to pay shipping and handling, which can sometimes cut into your savings.

See the next pages for the variety of discount sources available in this area.

SOURCES:

BOOKS AND PUBLICATIONS

AMERICAN FAMILY PUBLISHERS
P.O. Box 62111
Tampa, FL 33662-2111

1-800-237-2400

Magazine clearinghouses like American Family sell magazines at a big discount—up to 70% off newsstand prices. The reason? It's a relatively inexpensive way for magazines to get new subscribers, so some of the savings are passed on to you.

Outlet Type:	Mail order.
Product Line:	Broad selection of magazines—consumer and "popular" business. Limited selection of books, mostly popular reference and cookbooks.
Fax:	Not available.
Information:	Call or write to be put on the mailing list or to receive latest offer.
Orders Accepted By:	Mail, phone.
Payment:	Check, money order.
Delivery:	Magazines delivered via mail.
Guarantees:	Subscriptions can be canceled at any time.

BARNES & NOBLE BOOKSTORES, INC.
126 Fifth Avenue
Dept. 861F
New York, NY 10011

1-201-767-7079

Barnes & Noble's is a nationwide discounter of books, magazines, books on tape and other published materials. You can save up to 80% on overstocks, and routinely save 10–20% on just-published books and current magazines.

The good news is they also have a catalog operation that specializes in hard-to-find books, remainders and out-of-print books, including a full range of reference books. They also offer discounted books-on-tape, and some (generally nonbusiness) videos.

Outlet Type: Retail stores (call for location nearest you); Catalog house.

Product Line: Retail: full range of business books on all subjects, all at 10–20% off and more. Books on tape, reference books and more.
Catalog: hard-to-find, remaindered books, out-of-print books; savings range up to 80%. Good selection of reference books, although not many general business texts.

Fax: To receive catalog: 1-201-767-6638

Information: Catalog, phone.

Orders Accepted By: Phone, mail, fax.

Payment: MasterCard, Visa, American Express, Diners Club, Discover, check or money order.

Delivery: Shipping via 4th class mail or UPS ground service (delivery in 2–3 weeks); expedited handling available for $8 additional fee.

Guarantees: Satisfaction guaranteed. Returns are accepted.

DAEDALUS BOOKS, INC.
P.O. Box 9132
Hyattsville, MD 20781-0932

1-800-395-2665

Daedalus sells remaindered books at a tremendous discounts—50–90%. These are often ex-bestsellers from trade houses or high quality releases from university presses. Daedalus also sells current best sellers at 15% off list prices. It offers a good selection of "popular" business books.

Outlet Type:	Mail order.
Product Line:	Remaindered and current books from trade and university presses in a wide variety of subjects: fiction, children's, business, social sciences, philosophy and more.
Fax:	1–800–866–5578
Information:	Catalog. Price quote by phone or letter.
Orders Accepted By:	Phone, fax, mail.
Payment:	MasterCard, Visa, American Express, Optima, Discover, check or money order.
Delivery:	UPS ground service; 4th class mail to P.O. boxes.
Guarantees:	Satisfaction guaranteed. Returns accepted within 30 days.

EDWARD R. HAMILTON

Box 15-428
Falls Village, CT 06031

Telephone is unlisted

Edward R. Hamilton can save you up to 80% on recent overstocks, remainders, important and reprints from all major publishers in over 40 subject areas. They're a little more inconvenient to order from, because you have to request the catalog by mail (not phone) but their broad selection may make it worth your trouble, as they offer "more books by mail at lower prices than you'll find anywhere else."

Outlet Type:	Mail order only.
Product Line:	Recent and backlist books in a wide variety of subject areas, some as low as $1.95.
Fax:	Not available.
Information:	Catalog (free). Mail in your request.
Orders Accepted By:	Mail.

Payment:	MasterCard, Visa, money order.
Delivery:	48-hour shipment.
Guarantees:	Money back guarantee.

JESSICA'S BISCUIT

The Cookbook People
Box 301
Newtonville, MA 02160

1-800-878-4264
1-617-965-0530

We've included Jessica's Biscuit because it offers a great selection of books for restaurateurs and food managers. But the selection of cookbooks is great for anyone who likes to cook! The sale books in its catalog are the really special items—you can get discounts of up to 80%.

Outlet Type:	Mail order.
Product Line:	Books on cooking and food reference, including cookbooks, food handling, setting up a professional kitchen and various cuisines.
Fax:	1-617-527-0113
Information:	Catalog ($2).
Orders Accepted By:	Phone, fax, mail.
Payment:	MasterCard, Visa, money order.
Delivery:	UPS ground service. Next day delivery available at extra charge.
Guarantees:	Satisfaction guaranteed. Return goods within 90 days for full refund.

MAGAZINE MARKETPLACE

6523 North Galena Road
Peoria, IL 61632

1-309-691-4610

Magazine Marketplace offers a range of special interest magazines and more mainstream fare at savings up to 75% off publishers' rates. They are also a good source for discount nonfiction books, and they guarantee lowest pricing.

Outlet Type:	Mail order.
Product Line:	Magazines (special interest and general, including general business).
Fax:	1-309-689-3818
Information:	Phone, mailer.
Orders Accepted By:	Mail, fax.
Payment:	American Express, Visa, MasterCard, Discover, check or money order.
Delivery:	U.S. mail.
Guarantees:	Satisfaction guaranteed; returns up to 6 months from time of purchase. Lowest prices guaranteed.

Publisher's Clearing House

101 Winners Circle
Port Washington, NY 11050

1-800-645-9242
1-516-883-5432

Publisher's Clearing House is probably best known for its million-dollar sweepstakes, but the fact is that it can also save you up to 50% on a good selection of general business magazines. And who knows? You might actually win one of the prizes!

Outlet Type:	Mail order.
Product Line:	Broad variety of magazines, including mainstream business publications, at up to 50% off.
Fax:	Not available.
Information:	Periodic mailings.

Orders Accepted

By:	Mail.
Payment:	Check or money order. If you elect to use their installment plan, you can spread payments for your orders over 4 months.
Delivery:	U.S. mail.
Guarantees:	Satisfaction guaranteed.

THE REDDING GROUP, INC./REDDING'S AUDIO-BOOK SUPERSTORES

2300 North Scottsdale Road
Scottsdale, AZ 85257

1-602-BEST-SELLER (1-602-237-8355)

Business and motivational audiotapes are great things to listen to while you're driving from meeting to meeting, jogging or flying. The bad news is that they can cost upwards of $100—a hefty expense, particularly if you only listen to them once. But Redding offers you a way to get around that: They *rent* business and motivational tapes for only $4 a week, and business-related videos for $10 a week. Even though it's mail order, Redding makes it simple: Each tape comes with a preaddressed and prestamped return mailer. You get a full week's rental, starting when you receive the tape via priority mail, and ending when the return mailer is postmarked. The only sticky point is that you have to plan to use this service in order to rack up savings: Becoming a member will cost you about $20 per year—$10 for membership and $9.95 for the hefty catalog. (It contains over 15,000 titles in over 200 categories, including about 3500 business/motivational titles!) Note: If you're sitting with a lot of tapes you no longer listen to, you can trade them in for credit on future rentals. And you can get a $20 credit for referring a friend to Redding.

Outlet Type:	Retail store (located at address above) and catalog house.
Product Line:	3000–4000 audio books-on-tape and good selection of videos on business and motivational topics for rental or purchase.

Fax: Call the main telephone number listed above for
                     automatic switchover, or call 1-602-481-0076.

Information: Catalog ($9.95).

**Orders Accepted
By:**   Phone, fax, mail.

Payment: MasterCard, Visa, American Express, Discover,
                     check or money order. $100 refundable deposit is
                     required (cashed only if tapes are not returned).

Delivery: Priority mail.

Guarantees: Defective tapes will be replaced.

THE SCHOLAR'S BOOKSHELF

110 Melrich Road
Cranbury, NJ 08512

1-609-395-6933

By selling remaindered books published by university presses, The
Scholar's Bookshelf can save you 30–75% on "scholarly" books on general
business and technical subjects. They're also particularly strong on history.

Outlet Type: Catalog house.

Product Line: Scholarly and university press remaindered books
                     at a discount in a broad variety of subject areas.

Telephone: 1-609-395-6933

Fax: 1-609-395-0755

Information: Catalog.

**Orders Accepted
By:**   Mail, phone, fax.

Payment: MasterCard, Visa, check or money order.
                     Minimum order $10, $15 with credit card
                     purchase.

Delivery: U.S. mail.

Guarantees: Returns accepted within 30 days for exchange,
                     refund or credit.

STRAND BOOKSTORE, INC.

828 Broadway
New York, NY 10003

1-212-473-1452

Strand is very probably the largest used and out-of-print book dealer in the U.S., with 2.5 million titles and over 8 miles of books in its main retail outlet. If you can, you ought to visit its main store, as Strand encourages browsing and offers new books at 25–35% off, thousands of bargain-bin titles, and a wide range of hardcover "review copies" at 50% off. But if you can't get to New York, don't despair: Strand's "Specials" catalog, issued several times a year, can save you up to 80%. And you can call to request review copies of new bestsellers: If they have them, they'll send them to you at 50% off cover price.

Outlet Type:	Retail stores; catalog house.
Product Line:	New, used and rare books in virtually every subject category, many at deep discount.
Fax:	1-212-473-2591
Information:	Catalog or phone. Will conduct search of stock via fax request.
Orders Accepted By:	Mail, fax, phone.
Payment:	MasterCard, Visa, American Express, Discover, check or money order.
Delivery:	U.S. mail, UPS, Airborne Express. You pay shipping charges (minimum charge: $3.95); no additional handling charges.
Guarantees:	Returns accepted within 2 weeks of shipment for refund or credit.

3

Business Consulting Services

There's a saying: "Free advice is worth what you pay for it." The quality and variety of free or low-cost business consulting services available to U.S. businesses today puts the lie to that old adage, however.

Why would you want to use a consultant? There are lots of good reasons. Maybe you're just starting out, and you're not quite sure how to go about setting up your business. Or perhaps you're having a tough time making a go of it, and you'd like some help in getting the business back into the black. On the other hand, your business might be doing *so* well that you're having trouble managing its growth. You may need technical advice or counsel on how to arrange financing.

Whatever your reasons for seeking outside consulting assistance, there are a number of sources—government agencies, universities, trade associations and more—that you can access at minimal or no cost. We discuss the best of these consulting resources below.

Federal Government

The federal government offers a number of free or low-cost business consulting services through Small Business Administration (SBA) and Department of Commerce programs.

A couple of things to bear in mind as you attempt to use these programs:

- The federal government is a huge and confusing entity, even for those who work in it. Don't be discouraged if you reach someone who has never heard of the program you wish to explore—keep trying.
- A great program for finding your way through the governmental maze is *The Roadmap Program*. This is an information resource for all new and existing small businesses, and is invaluable in providing information, answers, contacts, government reports and additional sources of information. Contact: Roadmap, Office of Business Liaison, U.S. Department of Commerce, 14th and Constitution Avenue, N.W., Washington, D.C. 20230; telephone 1-202-482-2000.
- Another important information source are Federal Information Centers—entities set up to help citizens find out and take advantage of federal programs and services. If you have a question about a program but don't know which agency to contact, you can call or write your local FIC. They'll either get back to you or locate an expert who can answer your question. Call the national headquarters in Washington, D.C. at 1-800-346-3346 for the address and telephone number of the FIC nearest you.

Although it can be a little frustrating at first, the depth and scope of the consulting services offered by the federal government makes it worthwhile to go to the trouble of learning the ropes. Programs include:

- **SCORE/ACE:** Perhaps the largest and best known of the SBA programs is the Service Corps of Retired Executives (SCORE) and the Active Corps of Executives (ACE). In this program, retired or active executives with experience in your business offer free consulting advice and business guidance.
- **SBDCs:** Small Business Development Centers (SBDCs) are a cooperative effort of the SBA, universities, state and local governments and the private sector. They provide a host of free or low-cost management advisory services from more than 650 locations across the country.
- **SBI:** The Small Business Institute (SBI) provides management consulting to small businesses at no charge. Services are provided by seniors and graduate students from the country's leading business schools. There are hundreds of SBI locations across the country.
- **INCUBATORS:** Business "incubators" provide facilities and services to assist fledgling businesses start and grow. Operating as a coop-

erative effort of federal, state and local governments and the private sector, incubators provide qualified small businesses with free management, technical and financing consulting, as well as rent-free facilities and free or cooperative use of business equipment.

Please see the "Sources" section in this chapter for more information on these services and how to contact them.

State and Local Governments

There are myriad state and local programs that provide free or low-cost counseling to small businesses—taken together, many more programs than the federal government offers. However, they are often *less* well-publicized, which means that you will have to do some digging on your own. Bear in mind as you begin your search:

- Names of these services vary widely from locale to locale. You may have more luck describing the service you're looking for rather than using a name.
- Don't be surprised or fazed if the first person you talk to has never heard of the service. That doesn't necessarily mean it doesn't exist—it may be more evidence of "one hand not knowing what the other hand is offering." Keep trying.

In the "Sources" section of this chapter, we provide the names of the best centralized sources of information about what consulting help is available, including the main state agency that serves small businesses in each of the 50 states. These agencies are almost certain to have information on programs offering small businesses free or nominal-cost consulting and advice.

Local Government

Although we don't have the space to list local programs here, we urge you to take the time to check out what's available close to home. Most large U.S. cities provide assistance to small and/or new businesses, although what they're offering varies widely. It's worth it, however, to check out local programs to see if they include free or low-cost consulting. Here are some tips:

- Start with the city, county, or local government listings in your phone directory, and contact:

  Local Chambers of Commerce

  Economic Opportunity agencies

  Economic Development offices

  City/County Public Information offices

- Another good one-stop source is the U.S. Conference of Mayors, 1620 "Eye" Street, NW, Washington, DC 20006; telephone 1-202-293-7330. This organization collects information on a number (but not all) of city programs.

Some good news: Many of these agencies are set up to encourage investment in the area—so you don't always have to be a current resident to take advantage of a good number of these programs.

Minority and Women's Programs

If you're a member of a minority (African-American, Hispanic or American Indian), you can take advantage of a number of free/nominal-cost consulting services. These include:

- **MBDCs:** Minority Business Development Centers provide minority firms with advice and technical assistance on a low-cost fee basis. These services are provided by private firms who have been contracted by the Minority Business Development Agency to set up a Center. Currently, there are over 100 MBDCs in over 40 states and Puerto Rico.
- **MINORITY BUSINESS DEVELOPMENT AGENCY:** This government agency's charter is to provide assistance to minority-owned businesses. It provides a number of important services, including free management consulting. Consulting is provided mainly through the Regional and District offices of the MBDA.

For more information on minority programs, contact:

- Minority Business Development Agency (MBDA), U.S. Department of Commerce, Washington, D.C. 20230; telephone: 1-202-482-1936.
- Your state or local Minority Business Development agencies (names

may vary): see state and local government listings in your local telephone directory or contact your state's economic development office (see "Sources—State and Local" section in this chapter).

There are a number of good national women's programs, as well:

American Women's Economic Development Corp. ("AWED"): This organization provides women one-to-one, in-house and telephone counseling in virtually all phases of small business development and operations at very low cost.

Office of Women's Business Ownership, Small Business Administration: The Small Business Administration offers information, seminars and counseling through the Office of Women's Business Ownership, U.S. Small Business Administration, 409 3rd Street, SW, Washington, D.C. 20416; 1-202-205-6673.

Many states or cities have a women's directory (often called Women's White Pages" or "Women's Yellow Pages") that lists programs and contacts. Your local library may have a copy of this.

Many states have consulting programs for women-owned businesses. For more information on what is available in your state, contact the state agency that's responsible for economic development. We provide names, addresses and telephone numbers for each state in the "Sources" section, below.

If you can't locate local sources on your own, call the headquarters of the National Organization for Women ("NOW") at 1-202-331-0066, or your local NOW chapter.

Business School Programs

There are a number of ways in which you might tap into U.S. business schools to receive free business consulting advice.

- Many business schools allow their students to set up independent field studies, whereby students gain course credit for consulting to businesses. They perform this work under the supervision of a faculty advisor, so you're likely to get a good blend of enthusiasm (from the students) and experience (from the professor). Students usually perform this work at no charge, although you will usually be liable for out-of-pocket costs such as travel, long-distance phone calls and even report production.

- Many business schools have entrepreneur or small business clubs that may provide consulting services, or use your business as a case study for discussion.
- Universities often have courses of study focusing on small business or entrepreneurial subjects. You might check with them to see if you can tap into their students for some lower-cost consulting services.

See the following section for more information on what the nation's top business schools have to offer. Don't forget to check with your local colleges and universities.

As the above examples indicate, there are many sources of free or nominal-cost business consulting help available throughout the U.S. It's worth a little extra time and effort to give these avenues a try before you spend a significant amount on a private consultant.

SOURCES:

FREE/LOW COST CONSULTING

Federal Government

SCORE/ACE
Small Business Administration
1441 L Street, N.W.
Washington, D.C. 20416

1-800-827-5722 (SBA Answer Desk)
1-202-653-6768

Perhaps the largest and best-known of the SBA programs is the Service Corps of Retired Executives (SCORE) and the Active Corps of Executives (ACE). A nationwide service, SCORE/ACE consists of well over 12,000 volunteers: active or retired business people with real-life experience. Each user is paired with a volunteer who has relevant expertise in his or her industry.

That's not to say that SCORE and ACE are perfect. First, although many advisors really know their stuff, it's really luck of the draw. If you think you're not getting good advice, ask to be reassigned. Second, it may take effort on your part to even get an appointment, owing to limited SBA and SCORE/ACE staffing. Be persistent. Third, SCORE/ACE are reputedly more effective with basic business questions; if you're past the startup stage and are facing more complex problems, they may not be your best resource.

Having said that, SCORE and ACE still get high marks from many who have used them. And they have helped thousands upon thousands of small businesses start up and overcome hurdles.

Services Offered: Basic business advice; will check business plans, strategic marketing plans, financial plans; will give advice on obtaining loans.

Who's Eligible: Small businesses, as defined under SBA guidelines.

Cost:	Free.
Application:	In most locations, the initial contact does not require an appointment; however, some SCORE/ACE offices may have an appointment policy. Call the local SCORE/ACE office to check.
Other Tips:	SCORE/ACE publishes a number of informative booklets on running a small business. Call the Small Business Answer Desk at the 1-800 number above and just tell them what you need. They'll send it free of charge.

SMALL BUSINESS DEVELOPMENT CENTERS (SBDC)

Small Business Administration
1441 L Street, NW
Washington, D.C. 20416

1-800-827-5722 (SBA Answer Desk)
1-202-653-6768

Small Business Development Centers (SBDCs) are a cooperative effort of the SBA, universities, state and local governments and the private sector. Located at over 650 sites around the country, generally colleges and universities, SBDCs provide a broad variety of services, including low-cost seminars and workshops, management consulting through business school faculty and students, technical assistance, research studies and other types of specialized help.

SBDCs' overall mandate is to provide management training to small businesses, because the SBA estimates that "managerial deficiencies cause nine out of ten business failures."

Services Offered:	Management training and guidance for small businesses; basic business advice, business plan development, marketing, finance, legal issues, government procurement, exporting and more.
Who's Eligible:	Any small business owner or manager (small business as defined under SBA guidelines).
Cost:	Fees are modest—far less than you'd pay a private consulting firm for this level of quality and expertise.

Application: Contact the local SBDC in your area for
                         details.

THE SMALL BUSINESS INSTITUTE (SBI)
Small Business Administration
1441 L Street, NW
Washington, D.C. 20416

1-800-827-5722 (SBA Answer Desk)
1-202-606-4000

Small Business Institutes allows small business to benefit from consultation
and business advice given by graduate students and college seniors from the
leading business schools. Since many are on their way into the job market,
they tend to be very serious about the work and bring great energy to a
project. It's important for them to help your business work and to be able
to cite your success on their resumes. Moreover, the service takes place on
your premises, so it's convenient.

Services Offered: On-site management training and guidance for
                         small businesses; basic business advice, business
                         plan development, marketing, finance, legal issues,
                         government procurement, exporting and more.

Who's Eligible: Any small business owner or manager (small
                         business as defined under SBA guidelines).

Cost: Free.

Application: Contact local the local SBI in your area for details.
                         You can reach this through the local SBA office
                         (call the SBA Answer Desk for the office nearest
                         you or check the telephone directory).

BUSINESS INCUBATORS
c/o Office of Advocacy
Office of Private Sector Initiatives (OPSI)
Small Business Administration
1441 L Street, NW
Washington, D.C. 20416

1-202-331-9800

Business "incubators" provide facilities and services to assist fledgling businesses start and grow. Operating as a cooperative effort of federal, state and
local governments and the private sector, incubators provide qualified small

businesses with free management, technical and financing consulting, as well as rent-free facilities and free or cooperative use of business equipment. Note: Not every business is eligible, and the application process can be a lengthy and involved one. You'll have to write an application and provide a significant amount of documentation.

The SBA's Office of Private Sector Initiatives (OPSI) is the clearinghouse for incubator activity throughout the U.S. It can tell you what's going on around the country, and is an invaluable source of references and information, including a number of free publications that summarize ongoing initiatives, list the providers of incubator services and offer a step-by-step guide to accessing the incubator program. Of particular note is the publication, "Small Business Incubators," which is available free of charge from OPSI.

Services Offered: Business advice, free rent, free business equipment or no-cost use of business equipment, technical advice, assistance in acquiring loans/venture capital.

Who's Eligible: "Promising" businesses (your business must meet several performance and growth criteria). Criteria vary among incubators.

Cost: Nominal or free, if you qualify.

Application: Incubators are located throughout the country. Call OPSI, above, for information on those nearest you.

State and Local Sources

Although we don't have space to list all the sources of business advice and consulting at the state and local level, we have provided some centralized sources of information—both national and state-by-state. These include:

NATIONAL GOVERNOR'S ASSOCIATION
Hall of States
Suite 267
444 North Capitol Street, NW
Washington, D.C. 20001

1-202-624-5300

This group not only acts as a clearinghouse for information on the various programs available in states across the U.S., but it also can direct you to local and state sources (universities, associations and governmental agencies) that sponsor these programs.

Services Offered: Information on who's providing what programs at the state and local level.

Who's Eligible: Anyone may call for information.

Cost: Free (except for cost of call).

Application: Not applicable—information only.

Other Tips: Although this group has information on many programs, it is not an exhaustive, complete source.

STATE TECHNICAL ASSISTANCE CENTERS ("STACs")
c/o The Center for the Utilization of Federal Technology
National Technical Information Service
5285 Port Royal Road
Springfield, VA 22161

1-703-487-4600

If you're seeking technical consulting, STACs can offer assistance—and can also point you to other state, local and private sector programs that are aimed at boosting small companies' competitiveness. There are over 100 STACs in the U.S.; to find the one nearest you, ask for "State Technical Assistance Centers and Federal Technical Information Centers Available to U.S. Businesses," PR-767, available from The Center for the Utilization of Federal Technology (address above).

Services Offered: Technical consulting; technical and managerial assistance; technology transfer.

Who's Eligible: Anyone may call for information; STACs, however, are focused on firms that are using technology or are seeking to solve technology-related issues.

Cost: Consultation is generally free.

Application: Contact the STAC nearest you.

Other Tips: Don't forget to ask about other technology-related programs.

STATE-BY-STATE OFFICES OF ECONOMIC DEVELOPMENT

Address varies by state; see below for each state's address and telephone number.

These agencies will know of the myriad state and local programs available to help you and will be able to put you in touch with local sources. Below, we provide the names, addresses and telephone numbers of each state's economic development agency:

Services Offered: Information on who's providing what programs at the state and local level; assistance in accessing programs; help in obtaining loans and consulting advice

Who's Eligible: Anyone may call for information; actual programs may have restrictions. Programs are usually restricted to residents of the state or businesses locating in the state or local area.

Cost: Free (some programs may have fees attached).

Application: Not applicable—information only.

Other Tips: This should be your first stop to get information about consulting, financing, and other programs available for small businesses in your state.

See below for individual state information.

STATE-BY-STATE INFORMATION: ECONOMIC DEVELOPMENT OFFICES

ALABAMA DEVELOPMENT OFFICE
401 Adams Avenue, #600
Montgomery, AL 36130
1-205-242-0400

ALASKA DIVISION OF ECONOMIC
   DEVELOPMENT
Alaska Department of Commerce and
   Economic Development
P.O. Box 110804
Juneau, AK 99811-804
1-907-465-2018

ARIZONA OFFICE OF ECONOMIC
   DEVELOPMENT
Department of Commerce
3800 N. Central, Suite 1500
Phoenix, AZ 85012
1-602-280-1300

ARKANSAS INDUSTRIAL DEVELOPMENT
   COMMISSION
One State Capitol Mall
Little Rock, AR 72201
1-501-682-1121

CALIFORNIA DEPARTMENT OF
   COMMERCE
801 K Street, Suite 1700
Sacramento, CA 95814
1-916-322-1394

COLORADO OFFICE OF BUSINESS
   DEVELOPMENT
1625 Broadway, Suite 1710
Denver, CO 80202
1-303-892-3840

CONNECTICUT OFFICE OF SMALL
   BUSINESS SERVICES
Department of Economic
   Development
865 Brooks Street
Rocky Hill, CT 06067
1-203-258-4270

DELAWARE DEVELOPMENT OFFICE
99 Kings Highway
P.O. Box 1401
Dover, DE 19903
1-302-739-4271

DISTRICT OF COLUMBIA OFFICE OF
   BUSINESS AND ECONOMIC
   DEVELOPMENT
717 14th Street, NW, 10th Floor
Washington, D.C. 20005
1-202-727-6600

FLORIDA BUREAU OF BUSINESS
   ASSISTANCE
Department of Commerce
107 W. Gains Street
Collins Building, Room 443
Tallahassee, FL 32399-2000
1-904-488-9357

GEORGIA DEPARTMENT OF
   COMMUNITY AFFAIRS
1200 Equitable Building
100 Peachtree Street
Atlanta, GA 30303
1-404-656-6200

HAWAII SMALL BUSINESS
   INFORMATION SERVICE
Department of Business and Economic
   Development
Financial Assistance Branch
P.O. Box 2359
Honolulu, HI 96804
1-808-586-2600

IDAHO DEPARTMENT OF COMMERCE
Economic Development Division
700 West State Street
P.O. Box 83720
Boise, ID 83720-0093
1-208-334-2470

ILLINOIS DEPARTMENT OF COMMERCE
   AND COMMUNITY AFFAIRS
State of Illinois Center
100 West Randolph Street, Suite
   3-400
Chicago, IL 60601
1-312-814-7179

INDIANA SMALL BUSINESS
   ADMINISTRATION
429 N. Pennsylvania, Suite 100
Indianapolis, IN 46204-1873
1-317-226-7272

IOWA DEPARTMENT OF ECONOMIC
   DEVELOPMENT
200 East Grand Avenue
Des Moines, IA 50309
1-515-242-4700

KANSAS FIRST-STOP CLEARINGHOUSE
Existing Industry Development
   Division
Kansas Department of Commerce and
   Housing
700 Southwest Harrison Street, #1300
Topeka, KS 66603-3712
1-913-296-5298

KENTUCKY BUSINESS INFORMATION
  CLEARINGHOUSE
Cabinet for Economic Development
Department of Existing Business and
  Industry
2200 Capital Plaza Tower
Frankfort, KY 40601
1-502-564-4252

LOUISIANA DEPARTMENT OF
  ECONOMIC DEVELOPMENT
101 France Street, Suite 115
P.O. Box 94185
Baton Rouge, LA 70804-9185
1-504-342-3000

MAINE DEPARTMENT OF ECONOMIC
  AND COMMUNITY DEVELOPMENT
193 State Street
State House Station #59
Augusta, ME 04333
1-207-287-2656

MARYLAND BUSINESS ASSISTANCE
  CENTER
217 East Redwood Street, 10th Floor
Baltimore, MD 21202
1-800-654-7336 (Maryland only)
1-301-333-6975

MASSACHUSETTS OFFICE OF BUSINESS
  DEVELOPMENT
1 Ashburton Place, Room 2101
Boston, MA 02108
1-617-727-3221

MICHIGAN BUSINESS OMBUDSMAN
P.O. Box 30107
201 North Washington Square
Victor Office Center—4th Floor
Lansing, MI 48909
1-517-373-9808

MINNESOTA SMALL BUSINESS
  ASSISTANCE OFFICE
500 Metro Square
121 7th Place East
St. Paul, MN 55101-2146
1-612-296-3871

MISSISSIPPI DEPARTMENT OF
  ECONOMIC AND COMMUNITY
  DEVELOPMENT
P.O. Box 849
1200 Walter Sillers Building
Jackson, MS 39205
1-601-359-3449

MISSOURI BUSINESS ASSISTANCE
  CENTER
Department of Economic
  Development
P.O. Box 118
Jefferson City, MO 65102
1-314-751-4241

MONTANA DEPARTMENT OF
  COMMERCE
Director's Office
P.O. Box 200501
Helena, MT 59620-0501
1-406-444-3494

NEBRASKA DEPARTMENT OF ECONOMIC
  DEVELOPMENT
P.O. Box 94666
301 Centennial Mall South
Lincoln, NE 68509-4666
1-402-471-3782

NEVADA COMMISSION ON ECONOMIC
  DEVELOPMENT
Capitol Complex
Carson City, NV 89710
1-702-687-4325

NEW HAMPSHIRE DEPARTMENT OF
  RESEARCH AND ECONOMIC
  DEVELOPMENT
Office of Business and Industrial
  Development
Director, Division of Economic
  Development
172 Pembroke Road
P.O. Box 1856
Concord, NH 03302-1856
1-603-271-2591

NEW JERSEY OFFICE OF SMALL
  BUSINESS ASSISTANCE
Department of Commerce and
  Economic Development
20 West State, CN 835
Trenton, NJ 08625
1-609-292-3860

NEW MEXICO DEPARTMENT OF
  ECONOMIC DEVELOPMENT
Joseph Montoya Building
1100 St. Francis Drive
P.O. Box 20003
Santa Fe, NM 87503
1-505-827-0300

NEW YORK SMALL BUSINESS DIVISION
Department of Economic
  Development
One Commerce Plaza
Albany, NY 12245
1-518-474-7756

NORTH CAROLINA DEPARTMENT OF
  ECONOMIC AND COMMUNITY
  DEVELOPMENT
Business Industrial Development
430 North Salisbury Street
Raleigh, NC 27611
1-919-733-4151

NORTH DAKOTA CENTER FOR
  INNOVATION AND BUSINESS
  DEVELOPMENT
Box 8372
University Station
University of North Dakota
Grand Forks, ND 58202
1-701-777-3132

OHIO DEPARTMENT OF DEVELOPMENT
P.O. Box 1001
Columbus, OH 43266-0101
1-614-644-8748

OKLAHOMA—TEAMWORK OKLAHOMA
P.O. Box 26980
Oklahoma City, OK 73126-0980
1-405-843-9770

OREGON DEPARTMENT OF ECONOMIC
  DEVELOPMENT
775 Summer Street, NE
Salem, OR 97310
1-503-986-0155

PENNSYLVANIA BUREAU OF SMALL
  BUSINESS AND APPALACHIAN
  DEVELOPMENT
461 Forum Building
Harrisburg, PA 17120
1-717-783-5700

RHODE ISLAND GOOD NEIGHBOR
  ALLIANCE CORPORATION
15 Messenger Drive
Warwick, RI 02888
1-401-467-2880

SOUTH CAROLINA STATE
  DEVELOPMENT BOARD
P.O. Box 927
Columbia, SC 29202
1-803-737-0400

SOUTH DAKOTA GOVERNOR'S OFFICE
  OF ECONOMIC DEVELOPMENT
711 East Wells Avenue
Pierre, SD 57501-3369
1-800-872-6190

TENNESSEE OFFICE OF SMALL BUSINESS
Department of Economic and
  Community Development
Rachel Jackson State Office Building,
  7th Floor
320 Sixth Avenue North
Nashville, TN 37243-0405
1-615-741-2626

TEXAS DEPARTMENT OF COMMERCE
Small Business Division
Anson Jones Building
410 East Fifth Street
Austin, TX 78701
1-512-472-5059

UTAH SMALL BUSINESS DEVELOPMENT
  CENTER
102 W. 500 South, Suite 315
Salt Lake City, UT 84101-2315
1-801-581-7905

VERMONT ECONOMIC DEVELOPMENT
  DEPARTMENT
109 State Street
Montpelier, VT 05609
1-802-828-3221

VIRGINIA DEPARTMENT OF ECONOMIC
  DEVELOPMENT
Office of Small Business
P.O. Box 798
Richmond, VA 23206-0798
1-804-371-8252

WASHINGTON BUSINESS ASSISTANCE
  CENTER
Department of Trade and Economic
  Development
2001 Sixth Avenue, Suite 2700
Seattle, WA 98121
1-206-464-6282

WEST VIRGINIA SMALL BUSINESS
  DEVELOPMENT CENTER
1115 Virginia Street E.
Charleston, WV 25301
1-304-558-2960

WISCONSIN DEPARTMENT OF
  DEVELOPMENT
P.O. Box 7970
Madison, WI 53707
1-608-266-1018

WYOMING DIVISION OF ECONOMIC
  AND COMMUNITY DEVELOPMENT
Department of Commerce
Barrett Building, 4th Floor North
Cheyenne, WY 82002
1-800-262-3425

State-By-State Sources of Technology Consulting

Address varies by state. See Chapter 4, "Capital: Loans and Grants," for each state's address and telephone number.

Over half the states in the U.S. have set up programs to assist in technology transfer and to aid high-tech businesses. If your business is competing in a high-tech area, or is using technology to create a competitive edge, we suggest you contact your state's technology development office.

Services Offered: Help includes technical and managerial assistance, technology transfer, seed capital, venture capital, Small Business Innovative Research Grants (SBIRs) and Incubator programs.

Who's Eligible: Anyone may call for information; actual programs may have restrictions. Programs are usually restricted to residents of the state or businesses locating in the state or local area. Programs are also usually restricted to organizations competing in the high-tech arena or struggling with a technology issue.

Cost: Free (some programs may have fees attached).

Application: Not applicable—information only.

Other Tips: If your company uses technology or creates a high-tech product, these groups can put you in touch with myriad state and local programs.

See Chapter 4, "Capital: Loans and Grants," for individual state information.

Minority and Women's Services

There are a variety of sources of consulting assistance aimed at minorities and women. We've included the largest sources below, but don't forget about state and local programs. The best way to find out about these programs is to call your state's economic development office. (We've included the numbers for each state above, in "State and Local Sources".) Other important sources:

MINORITY BUSINESS DEVELOPMENT CENTERS

Assistant Director
Office of Program Operations
Room 5063
Minority Business Development Agency
U.S. Department of Commerce
14th and Constitution Avenue, NW
Washington, D.C. 20230

1-202-482-1936 (see below for local numbers)

There are approximately 100 MBDCs across the U.S. The purpose of these centers is to provide business development services for a minimal fee to minority firms and individuals interested in entering, expanding or improving their efforts in the marketplace.

Services Offered: MBDC operators provide a wide range of services to clients, from initial consultation to the identification and resolution of specific business problems. Advice includes: preparing financial packages, business counseling, business information and management, accounting guidance, marketing, business/industrial site analysis, production, engineering, construction assistance, procurement and identification of potential business opportunities.

Who's Eligible: Existing minority-owned businesses, and minorities interested in starting a business.

Cost: Low cost (below market); sometimes free.

Application: Apply to your local MBDC.

Other Tips: To find out if you qualify, and what these services include, contact the MBDC office nearest you for more information. Offices include:

Atlanta	1-404-586-0973	(Regional)
Boston	1-617-723-4216	(District)
Chicago	1-312-567-6061	(Regional)
Dallas	1-214-767-8001	(Regional)
Kansas City	1-816-471-1520	(District)
Miami	1-306-591-7355	(District)
New York	1-212-264-4743	(Regional)
Philadelphia	1-215-597-9236	(District)
Wash., D.C.	1-202-785-2886	(Regional)

AMERICAN WOMEN'S ECONOMIC DEVELOPMENT CORP. ("AWED")

71 Vanderbilt Avenue, Suite 320
New York, NY 10165

1-212-692-9100

230 Pine Avenue, 3rd Floor
Long Beach, CA 90802

1-310-983-3747

1250 24th Street, NW
Room 120
Washington, D.C. 20037

1-202-857-0091 (DC)

This organization provides women one-to-one, in-house and telephone counseling in virtually all phases of small business development and operations at very low cost.

Services Offered: Experienced counselors can offer guidance to women thinking of starting a business or to women business owners facing specific problems.

Who's Eligible: Women-owned businesses.

Cost: Counseling sessions (1.5 hours) cost $25 for AWED members and $35 for nonmembers; AWED membership is $55 per year.

Application: Call the national headquarters, above. There are a number of other AWED offices throughout the U.S.

Other Tips: AWED gets high marks from those we spoken to for the quality of its consulting.

OFFICE OF WOMEN'S BUSINESS OWNERSHIP. SMALL BUSINESS ADMINISTRATION
409 3rd Street, SW
Washington, D.C. 20416

1-202-205-6673

The Small Business Administration recognizes that women may have special needs when it comes to developing and managing a business. Accordingly, the SBA has set up the Office of Women's Business Ownership, a network of almost 100 offices nationwide that are focused on women's business needs. Contact the main number for the name of the SBA representative nearest you, or call the local SBA office.

Services Offered: Provides women information, seminars and counseling on a variety of topics, including getting financing, doing business with the U.S. government and mentoring programs.

Who's Eligible: Women-owned businesses.

Cost: Nominal fees or free.

Application: Call the national office, above, or your local SBA office.

Other Tips: Don't forget to ask about the Women's Entrepreneurial Lunch programs. The SBA runs these programs in almost every major city. And the mentoring program, which pairs experienced women business owners with those just starting out, is terrific if you need an ongoing sounding board and "good example" when things get tough.

Business School Programs

There are a number of university and college programs that allow you access to some of the nation's brightest minds: its students. If you're interested in taking advantage of this option, we strongly suggest that you contact the institutions of higher learning in your area—preferably, those with graduate business schools.

We have by no means gathered an extensive list. To give you a flavor of what's available, however, we've checked with some of the nation's top business schools. This is what we found:

- *Harvard Graduate School of Business* allows its second-year students to perform independent field studies. But be aware: Although students receive no remuneration, you will be responsible for covering their out-of-pocket costs. And since students are free to choose the study they wish to do, there's no guarantee they'll choose yours. Finally, most of these studies take place in the Spring, so if you need consulting immediately, the timing may not be right. Call the school at 1-617-495-5000 for more information on how to submit your project.
- *Stanford University Graduate School of Business* has a club, the "Business Development Association" that offers support and assistance to startup ventures. Contact the club at 1-415-723-9208.

- *Vanderbilt University* offers a course, "Interactive Applied Projects," where business school students work with a company on a specific project and receive course credit. For more information on this program, contact Professor Rick Oliver at 1-615-322-2534.
- *MIT's Sloan School of Business* has various student clubs that may offer free consulting assistance, including the Volunteer Consulting Group and the New Ventures Association. For more information, contact 1-617-253-3730.
- *The University of Pennsylvania's Wharton School* offers no formal courses, but has two student clubs, the Small Business Center and the Entrepreneurial Center. For more information on these clubs, call 1-215-898-3030.

These are just a sampling of the available programs. For more information, contact the business schools in your area.

4

Capital: Loans and Grants

Whether you're starting a business or growing an existing one, chances are good that, at some point, you'll need a capital infusion. This chapter discusses the different options available to small businesses, from banks to government sources to private foundations.

Bank Loans

Typically, when a small business needs money, the first place they turn to is a bank. Although it's true that banks are a tried-and-true source of funds, you should be aware that there are some drawbacks:

- *Access and cost.* It's an unfortunate statistic that many small businesses fail—unfortunate because this not only makes banks wary of making small business loans at all, but it also results in higher interest rates on these loans. If you're lucky enough to get a loan, you may end up paying a significant premium over prime rate.
- *Cash flow woes.* Usually, you have to start paying back a bank loan in thirty days. If you're just starting out, that's usually far sooner than your business is actually generating any cash! That alone can sink your business before it gets launched.
- *Bank inflexibility.* Although you can always attempt to negotiate a lower interest rate or other fee reductions—and usually succeed—the

extent of lending officers' flexibility is stymied by bank requirements. And often, bank policy demands that business loans be secured by your personal assets, something best avoided for your financial well-being.

Despite these issues, banks account for the majority of business loans. So choosing the right bank and positioning your business in the most positive light are critical both in getting the loan and in obtaining a favorable rate. Experts suggest these tips:

- *Pick a bank that wants to lend.* Check the bank's financial strength. A shaky bank is often reluctant to make riskier small business loans, and is more likely to call your loan if their prospects sour. What's more, a bank that's been burned by a lot of bad loans is going to be tight on credit and inflexible in its lending policies. On the other hand, a bank with a high deposit-to-loan ratio will *want* to make loans. (Remember, it needs to keep its money working to make more money.) Also, determine the bank's legal lending limit and find one whose ceiling is at least twice your company's current funding needs. You can find this out by checking the bank's quarterly Statement of Conditions, or by asking the loan officer.
- *Avoid large, nonlocal banks.* Otherwise, your loan application is usually scrutinized by a bunch of out-of-town number crunchers who don't know you or your business—and will nix the loan rather than take the time to discuss things with you.
- *Chemistry and experience counts.* Your loan officer should be interested in you and your business—and he or she should have the perspective that experience brings. Has the loan officer made prior loans in your industry? Experienced a recession? Had a significant amount of experience with that bank? The more your officer knows, the more reasonable he or she is likely to be. Inexperience breeds insecurity, and hence, inflexibility.
- *Put your best foot forward.* Your job is to convince the loan officer that your company is a good bet for a loan. So be professional. Know exactly how much money you'll need, and be able to state succinctly what it's for. If it's for a new product or service, bring the marketing plan. If it's for new equipment, be prepared to show why it's necessary and what benefits it will bring to your operations. Also key: Clean up any issues at credit rating agencies before you begin discussions. Key credit bureaus are:

    Dun & Bradstreet   1-800-333-0505
    Equifax   1-800-685-1111

Trans Union   1-216-779-7200
TRW   1-800-682-7654

Don't accept unfavorable terms. Apart from too-high interest, you'll want to focus on the repayment schedule. The bank will want a short repayment schedule that gives them more opportunities to pull out of the financing, but you want a longer one. Another thing to focus on is the collateral. Try hard to avoid pledging personal assets, although this won't always be possible.

- *Look for a bank that will link loan cost to your performance.* If you're sure that your business's performance is heading up, negotiate "performance-based pricing" for your loan rate. This simply means that as your business does better (typically measured in debt-to-equity ratio) the bank's risk gets lower—and this lower risk is then reflected in a lower rate. Although you may not be able to negotiate *specific* rate reductions at the time you obtain your loan, you and your bank should be able to agree, in principle, to relax your loan terms or reduce your interest rate. Note: This can be a Pandora's box, as banks will often demand the right to get higher rates if your performance sours.

Nonbank Sources of Money

Sometimes you can't avoid taking a loan from a bank. But there are other options to access low-cost money—and, wonder of wonders, obtain grants that you don't have to repay at all:

- *Check out private financing.* If you know individuals who are looking for a good investment, approach them. If you don't know of any, ask your stock broker, lawyer or accountant. Or put an advertisement in a trade journal, newspaper or magazine aimed at entrepreneurs or investors. Private investors can be far more flexible with their terms—so that, for instance, you can arrange a payment schedule that doesn't suck your cash flow dry in the first two years.
- *Don't forget the U.S. government.* In recent years, the annual value of the U.S. government's grants, loans and loan guarantees has exceeded $100 billion, and the number of awards tops three million. Your first stop in finding government-sponsored loans and grants should be the Small Business Administration, which administers many (but certainly not all) of the federal funding programs aimed at small businesses. We include the largest SBA programs in the "Sources" section.

At the same time, remember that there are many *other* federal sources for loans and grants. Many loans and grants are focused on industries under the aegis of a specific agency. For instance, did you know that:

In 1994, the Department of Agriculture had $17 million in grant money to fund research to develop new nonfood, nonfeed products that could be produced from agricultural commodities? Or that it makes available Small Business Innovation Research grants (historically averaging $91,250) that are given to stimulate innovation in the private sector and are limited to businesses of under 500 employees?

The National Oceanic and Atmospheric Administration makes grants to individuals and small businesses to help enhance fisheries?

The Maritime Administration of the Department of Transportation provides guaranteed/insured loans to cover 75% of the cost of building a ship? They also provide direct grants and tax abatements.

The Department of Energy makes grants (averaging $83,000) to encourage innovation in developing nonnuclear energy technology, and small businesses, individual inventors and entrepreneurs are "especially invited" to participate?

The Overseas Private Investment Corporation will guarantee loans made by U.S. investors in developing countries?

If you're seeking funding for a project or for a business, it's worth contacting the agency that has jurisdiction over the industry in which you're operating. We provide sources of some key loan/grant programs in the "Sources" section in this chapter, but please note that this is incomplete. For more information, good compilations are "Government Giveaways For Entrepreneurs II" by Matthew Lesko (Information USA, Inc., 1994) or the "Catalog of Federal Domestic Assistance" (U.S. Government Printing Office, Washington, D.C.; 1-202-512-0000). "Government Giveaways" has the added benefit of including state, minority and other programs.

• *State money is available, too.* Every state provides loans or program grants to small businesses, as well as a number of other consulting and business procurement assistance programs. To discover what's out there, we suggest you start with your state's economic development office. (We provide telephone numbers for each state in the Sources section.) Additional sources: the National Governors' Association

(Hall of States, 444 North Capitol Street, NW, Washington, D.C. 20009; telephone 1-202-624-5300), which acts as a clearinghouse for information on the various programs available in states across the U.S., and the book "Government Giveaways For Entrepreneurs II" by Matthew Lesko (Information USA, Inc., 1994), which lists state-by-state programs and resources.

- *Local governments sometimes have loan programs.* Don't forget to find low-cost sources of funding right at your front door. Most large U.S. cities provide assistance to small and/or new businesses, although what they're offering varies widely. To get to them, start with the city, county, or local government listings in your phone directory, and contact:

  - Local chambers of commerce
  - Economic opportunity agencies
  - Economic development offices
  - City/county public information offices

Another source: the U.S. Conference of Mayors, 1620 Eye Street, NW, Washington, D.C. 20006; telephone 1-202-293-7330. This organization collects information on a number of (but not all) city programs.

- *Private foundations are another, often underutilized, source of funding.* A foundation will often provide outright grants, low-cost loans, letters of credit or consulting services to small businesses that are engaged in activities that further the foundation's charitable goals. Sometimes they will make this assistance available directly to a small business ("Program Related Investment"); sometimes they will only provide money to a nonprofit organization that then turns around and gives the money to a small business ("Flow Through Funding"). Either way, foundations can be an important source of funding—particularly for small businesses focused on socially-beneficial activities, owned by minorities or located in economically-depressed areas. Some key points:

  - Grants are often available only for a particular industry or type of business.
  - There are often, but not always, geographic restrictions on who might apply, e.g., just businesses in California, or just companies focused on improving health care in South Eddy County, New Mexico.

If you're a woman, or a minority, there are numerous federal and state grant and loan programs for you.

- The Small Business Administration does not set aside loan money specifically for women-owned businesses, but it does offer a small number of grants, as well as information, seminars and counseling through the Office of Women's Business Ownership, U.S. Small Business Administration, 409 3rd Street, SW, Washington, D.C. 20416; 1-202-205-6673.
- The U.S. Department of Commerce runs approximately 100 Minority Business Development Centers throughout the U.S. whose purpose is to provide management and technical assistance to minority clients at nominal fees. MBDCs do not make loans to small businesses—instead, they provide funds to consultants who work with you on your business problems, including obtaining funding and government business. The program seems to work: In 1992, MBDC clients obtained $360 million in financial packages and $877 million in procurement contracts.
- Many states have loan programs for minority or women-owned businesses. For more information on what is available in your state, contact the state agency that's responsible for economic development. We provide names, addresses and telephone numbers for each state in the "Sources" section, below.

SOURCES:

OBTAINING LOW-COST CAPITAL

Federal Government: SBA Programs

SMALL BUSINESS ADMINISTRATION
409 3rd Street, SW
Washington, D.C. 20416

1-800-827-5722 (Answer Desk)

The SBA administers many of the loan, guaranteed loan, grant and direct payment programs for small businesses nationwide. Below, we list some of the largest SBA programs. Note: There are other programs too, aimed at minorities, veterans, women and disaster relief. For more information about other programs, call the SBA Answer Desk (it's toll-free!), contact your local SBA office (there are over 100 throughout the U.S.) or check "Government Giveaways For Entrepreneurs II" by Matthew Lesko (Information USA, Inc., 1994) or the "Catalog of Federal Domestic Assistance" (U.S. Government Printing Office, Washington, D.C.; 1-202-512-1800).

There are over 100 local SBA offices throughout the U.S. Because SBA loans are approved at the local level, it makes sense to contact and visit your local SBA office early on in your loan application process. There, they can answer your questions, give you the forms and tell you what other assistance they may have available.

SBA PROGRAM: SMALL BUSINESS LOANS (REGULAR BUSINESS LOANS—7(A) LOANS)
Director
Loan Policy and Procedures Branch
Small Business Administration
409 3rd Street, SW
Washington, D.C. 20416

1-202-205-6493

This, a guaranteed loan program, is the largest SBA offering, having made available over $5 billion in loans in 1992. The government doesn't actually lend you the money; instead, it guarantees payment (usually, 70% of the loan is covered) to the lender in case of default. With the U.S. government assuming most of the risk, you can obtain the financing you need. The money is flexible, as it can be used for working capital, real estate, refinancing or equipment. But there are some issues: Uncle Sam levies a fee to make these loans (about 2%) and banks typically charge substantially higher interest—about a point higher than regular commercial loans.

If you do decide to go for an SBA loan, bear in mind that *selecting the lender is a key decision*. You want one of the 200 lenders who has earned "Preferred" status from the SBA, because that gives them the ability to approve your loan request on the spot. Obtain a list of "Preferred" lenders from your local SBA office.

Financing Type: Guaranteed loan.

Who's Eligible: Most small business who have been unable to obtain financing in the private credit marketplace. Businesses must be able to demonstrate ability to repay loan.

Restrictions: Loan limit: $750,000. Not available for not-for-profit organizations, or companies in real estate, investment or businesses involved in the creation or distribution of ideas (e.g., newspapers). Businesses must be within a certain size (varies for different types of industries).

Funds Available: In 1993, $5 billion.

SBA PROGRAM: CERTIFIED DEVELOPMENT LOANS (504 LOANS)

Office of Economic Development
Small Business Administration
409 3rd Street, SW
Washington, D.C. 20416

1-202-205-6485

This is a guaranteed loan program that allows small businesses to finance the cost of fixed assets. Essentially, the government guarantees payment of debentures the small business sells to private investors.

Financing Type: Guaranteed/insured loan.

Who's Eligible: Small businesses independently owned and run for profit.

Restrictions: Loans are to assist businesses in the acquisition of major fixed assets, including land, buildings, and equipment. Loans are long-term (10- or 20-year).

Funds Available: In 1993, $700 million (est.).

SBA PROGRAM: SMALL BUSINESS INVESTMENT COMPANIES

Director
Office of Investments
Small Business Administration
409 3rd Street, SW
Washington, D.C. 20416

1-202-205-6510

This program establishes investment companies, who in turn provide management and financial assistance on a continuing basis to eligible small business concerns. Financial assistance is provided by making long-term loans and/or by the purchase of debt or equity type securities in the small businesses.

Financing Type: Direct loans/guaranteed/insured loans.

Who's Eligible: Individual businesses which meet the SBA's criteria of a "small business."

Restrictions: For some programs (Specialty Small Business Investment Companies, or SSBICs), businesses must be owned and operated by socially or economically disadvantaged individuals.

Funds Available: In 1993, over $100 million in guaranteed loans.

SBA PROGRAM: 8(A) PROGRAM LOANS

Director
Loan Policy and Procedures Branch
Small Business Administration
409 3rd Street
Washington, D.C. 20416

1-202-205-6570

This program provides direct and guaranteed loans to small businesses owned by socially and economically disadvantaged persons. Loans are used for capital improvements and working capital.

Financing Type: Direct loans/guaranteed loans.

Who's Eligible: Small businesses owned by socially and economically disadvantaged persons.

Restrictions: Business must also be receiving assistance under SBA Programs 7(J) or 8(A), and must demonstrate an ability to repay the loan.

Funds Available: In 1992, $4.8 million in loans were made.

Federal Government: Other Sources of Funding

In addition to the SBA, other federal government agencies provide a variety of loan, grant and guaranteed loan programs. We suggest you contact the following to determine whether you are eligible for their programs:

U.S. DEPARTMENT OF AGRICULTURE
14th and Independence Avenue, SW
Washington, D.C. 20250
1-202-720-2791

U.S. DEPARTMENT OF COMMERCE
14th and Constitution Avenue, NW
Washington, D.C. 20230
1-202-482-2000

U.S. DEPARTMENT OF HOUSING AND
   URBAN DEVELOPMENT
451 7th Street, SW
Washington, D.C. 20410
1-202-708-1422

U.S. DEPARTMENT OF HEALTH AND
   HUMAN SERVICES
200 Independence Avenue, SW
Washington, D.C. 20210
1-202-619-0257

U.S. DEPARTMENT OF
   TRANSPORTATION
800 Independence Ave., SW
Washington, D.C. 20590
1-202-366-4000

NATIONAL ENDOWMENT FOR THE ARTS
1100 Pennsylvania Avenue, NW
Washington, D.C. 20506
1-202-682-5400

NATIONAL SCIENCE FOUNDATION
Small Business Innovation Project
4201 Wilson Boulevard
Room 570
Arlington, VA 22230
1-703-306-1234

ENVIRONMENTAL PROTECTION AGENCY
401 M Street, SW
Washington, D.C. 20460
1-202-260-2090

OVERSEAS PRIVATE INVESTMENT
  CORPORATION (OPIC)
1100 New York Avenue, NW
Washington, D.C. 20527
1-202-336-8400

U.S. DEPARTMENT OF ENERGY
Forrestal Building
1000 Independence Avenue, SW
Washington, D.C. 20585
1-202-586-5000

U.S. DEPARTMENT OF EDUCATION
400 Maryland Avenue, SW
Washington, D.C. 20202
1-202-708-5366

State Government

STATE-BY-STATE OFFICES OF ECONOMIC DEVELOPMENT

Address varies by state; see below for each state's address and telephone number.

These agencies will know of the myriad state and local loan, grant and seed money programs available to you, and will be able to put you in touch with local sources. Below, we provide the names, addresses and telephone numbers of each state's economic development agency:

Services Offered: Information on who's providing what programs at the state and local level; assistance in accessing programs; help in obtaining loans and consulting advice.

Who's Eligible: Anyone may call for information; actual programs may have restrictions. Programs are usually restricted to residents of the state or businesses located in the state or local area.

Cost: Free (some programs may have fees attached).

Application: Not applicable—information only.

Other Tips: This should be your first stop to get information about consulting, financing and other programs available for small businesses in your state.

See below for individual state information.

STATE BY STATE INFORMATION: ECONOMIC DEVELOPMENT OFFICES

ALABAMA DEVELOPMENT OFFICE
401 Adams Avenue, #600
Montgomery, AL 36130
1-205-242-0400

ALASKA DIVISION OF ECONOMIC
   DEVELOPMENT
Alaska Department of Commerce and
   Economic Development
P.O. Box 110804
Juneau, AK 99811-804
1-907-465-2018

ARIZONA OFFICE OF ECONOMIC
   DEVELOPMENT
Department of Commerce
3800 N. Central, Suite 1500
Phoenix, AZ 85012
1-602-280-1300

ARKANSAS INDUSTRIAL DEVELOPMENT
   COMMISSION
One State Capitol Mall
Little Rock, AR 72201
1-501-682-1121

CALIFORNIA DEPARTMENT OF
   COMMERCE
801 K Street, Suite 1700
Sacramento, CA 95814
1-916-322-1394

COLORADO OFFICE OF BUSINESS
   DEVELOPMENT
1625 Broadway, Suite 1710
Denver, CO 80202
1-303-892-3840

CONNECTICUT OFFICE OF SMALL
   BUSINESS SERVICES
Department of Economic
   Development
865 Brooks Street
Rocky Hill, CT 06067
1-203-258-4270

DELAWARE DEVELOPMENT OFFICE
99 Kings Highway
P.O. Box 1401
Dover, DE 19903
1-302-739-4271

DISTRICT OF COLUMBIA OFFICE OF
   BUSINESS AND ECONOMIC
   DEVELOPMENT
717 14th Street, NW, 12th Floor
Washington, D.C. 20005
1-202-727-6600

FLORIDA BUREAU OF BUSINESS
   ASSISTANCE
Department of Commerce
107 W. Gains Street
Collins Building, Room 443
Tallahassee, FL 32399-2000
1-904-488-9357

GEORGIA DEPARTMENT OF
   COMMUNITY AFFAIRS
1200 Equitable Building
100 Peachtree Street
Atlanta, GA 30303
1-404-656-6200

HAWAII SMALL BUSINESS
   INFORMATION SERVICE
Department of Business and Economic
   Development—Financial Assistance
   Branch
P.O. Box 2359
Honolulu, HI 96804
1-808-586-2600

IDAHO DEPARTMENT OF COMMERCE
Economic Development Division
700 West State Street
Joe R. Williams Building
P.O. Box 83720
Boise, ID 83720-0093
1-208-334-2470

ILLINOIS DEPARTMENT OF COMMERCE
AND COMMUNITY AFFAIRS
James R. Thompson Center
100 West Randolph Street
Suite 3-400
Chicago, IL 60601
1-312-814-7179

INDIANA SMALL BUSINESS
ADMINISTRATION
429 N. Pennsylvania, Suite 100
Indianapolis, IN 46204-1873
1-317-226-7272

IOWA DEPARTMENT OF ECONOMIC
DEVELOPMENT
200 East Grand Avenue
Des Moines, IA 50309
1-515-242-4700

KANSAS FIRST-STOP CLEARINGHOUSE
Kansas Department of Commerce and
Housing
Existing Industry Division
700 Southwest Harrison Street
Suite 1300
Topeka, KS 66603-3712
1-913-296-5298

KENTUCKY BUSINESS INFORMATION
CLEARINGHOUSE
Cabinet for Economic Development
Department of Existing Business and
Industry
2100 Capital Plaza Tower
Frankfort, KY 40601
1-502-564-4252

LOUISIANA DEPARTMENT OF
ECONOMIC DEVELOPMENT
101 France Street, Suite 115
P.O. Box 94185
Baton Rouge, LA 70804-9185
1-504-342-3000

MAINE DEPARTMENT OF ECONOMIC
AND COMMUNITY DEVELOPMENT
193 State Street
State House Station #59
Augusta, ME 04333
1-207-287-2656

MARYLAND BUSINESS ASSISTANCE
CENTER
217 East Redwood Street, 10th Floor
Baltimore, MD 21202
1-301-333-6975
1-800-654-7336 (Maryland only)

MASSACHUSETTS OFFICE OF BUSINESS
DEVELOPMENT
1 Ashburton Place, Room 2101
Boston, MA 02108
1-617-727-3221

MICHIGAN BUSINESS OMBUDSMAN
201 North Washington Square
Victor Office Center
4th Floor
Lansing, MI 48913
1-517-373-9808

MINNESOTA SMALL BUSINESS
ASSISTANCE OFFICE
500 Metro Square
121 Seventh Place East
St. Paul, MN 55101-2146
1-612-296-3871

MISSISSIPPI DEPARTMENT OF
ECONOMIC AND COMMUNITY
DEVELOPMENT
1200 Walter Sillers Building
550 High Street
Jackson, MS 39201
1-601-359-3449

MISSOURI BUSINESS ASSISTANCE
  CENTER
Department of Economic
  Development
P.O. Box 118
Jefferson City, MO 65102
1-800-523-1434

MONTANA DEPARTMENT OF
  COMMERCE
1424 Ninth Avenue
Helena, MT 59620
1-406-444-3494

NEBRASKA DEPARTMENT OF ECONOMIC
  DEVELOPMENT
P.O. Box 94666
301 Centennial Mall South
Lincoln, NE 68509-4666
1-402-471-3782

NEVADA COMMISSION ON ECONOMIC
  DEVELOPMENT
5151 South Carson Street
Carson City, NV 89710
1-702-687-4325

NEW HAMPSHIRE DEPARTMENT OF
  RESEARCH AND ECONOMIC
  DEVELOPMENT
Office of Business and Industrial
  Development
Director, Division of Economic
  Development
172 Pembroke Road
P.O. Box 1856
Concord, NH 03302-1856
1-603-271-2591

NEW JERSEY OFFICE OF SMALL
  BUSINESS ASSISTANCE
Department of Commerce and
  Economic Development
20 West State, CN 835
Trenton, NJ 08625
1-609-292-3860

NEW MEXICO DEPARTMENT OF
  ECONOMIC DEVELOPMENT
Joseph Montoya Building
1100 St. Francis Drive
Santa Fe, NM 87503
1-505-827-0300

NEW YORK SMALL BUSINESS DIVISION
Department of Economic
  Development
One Commerce Plaza
Albany, NY 12245
1-518-474-7756

NORTH CAROLINA DEPARTMENT OF
  ECONOMIC AND COMMUNITY
  DEVELOPMENT
Business Industrial Development
430 North Salisbury Street
Raleigh, NC 27611
1-919-733-4151

NORTH DAKOTA CENTER FOR
  INNOVATION AND BUSINESS
  DEVELOPMENT
Box 8372
University of North Dakota
Grand Forks, ND 58202
1-701-777-3132

OHIO DEPARTMENT OF DEVELOPMENT
P.O. Box 1001
Columbus, OH 43266-0101
1-614-644-8748

OKLAHOMA—TEAMWORK OKLAHOMA
P.O. Box 26980
Oklahoma City, OK 73126-0980
1-405-843-9770

OREGON DEPARTMENT OF ECONOMIC
  DEVELOPMENT
775 Summer Street, NE
Salem, OR 97310
1-503-986-0155

PENNSYLVANIA BUREAU OF SMALL
  BUSINESS AND APPALACHIAN
  DEVELOPMENT
461 Forum Building
Harrisburg, PA 17120
1-717-783-5700

RHODE ISLAND GOOD NEIGHBOR
  ALLIANCE CORPORATION
15 Messenger Drive
Warwick, RI 02888
1-401-467-2880

SOUTH CAROLINA STATE
  DEVELOPMENT BOARD
P.O. Box 927
Columbia, SC 29202
1-803-737-0400

SOUTH DAKOTA GOVERNOR'S OFFICE
  OF ECONOMIC DEVELOPMENT
711 East Wells Avenue
Pierre, SD 57501-3369
1-800-872-6190

TENNESSEE OFFICE OF SMALL BUSINESS
Department of Economic and
  Community Development
Rachel Jackson State Office Building
320 Sixth Avenue North
7th Floor
Nashville, TN 37243-0405
1-615-741-2626

TEXAS DEPARTMENT OF COMMERCE
Small Business Division
Anson Jones Building
410 East 5th Street
P.O. Box 12728
Austin, TX 78701
1-512-472-5059

UTAH SMALL BUSINESS DEVELOPMENT
  CENTER
102 W. 500 South, Suite 315
Salt Lake City, UT 84101-2315
1-801-581-7905

VERMONT ECONOMIC DEVELOPMENT
  DEPARTMENT
109 State Street
Montpelier, VT 05609
1-802-828-3221

VIRGINIA DEPARTMENT OF ECONOMIC
  DEVELOPMENT
Office of Small Business
P.O. Box 798
Richmond, VA 23206-0798
1-804-371-8252

WASHINGTON BUSINESS ASSISTANCE
  CENTER
Department of Community Trade and
  Economic Development
2001 Sixth Avenue, Suite 2700
Seattle, WA 98121
1-206-464-6282

WEST VIRGINIA SMALL BUSINESS
  DEVELOPMENT CENTER
1115 Virginia Street E
Charleston, WV 25301
1-304-558-2960

WISCONSIN DEPARTMENT OF
  DEVELOPMENT
P.O. Box 7970
Madison, WI 53707
1-608-266-1018

WYOMING DIVISION OF ECONOMIC
  AND COMMUNITY DEVELOPMENT
Department of Commerce
Barrett Building, 4th Floor North
Cheyenne, WY 82002
1-800-262-3425

STATE-BY-STATE SOURCES: TECHNOLOGY CONSULTING

Address varies by state; see below for each state's address and telephone number.

Over half the states in the U.S. have set up programs to assist in technology transfer and to aid high-tech businesses. This help often extends to seed capital, grants, loans or loan guarantees. If your business is competing in a high-tech area, or is using technology to create a competitive edge, we suggest you contact your state's technology development office. We include the address and telephone number of each state's main office below.

Services Offered: Help includes seed capital, venture capital, Small Business Innovative Research Grants (SBIRs), Incubator programs, technical and managerial assistance and technology transfer.

Who's Eligible: Anyone may call for information; actual programs may have restrictions. Programs are usually restricted to residents of the state or businesses locating in the state or local area. Programs are also usually restricted to organizations competing in the high-tech arena or struggling with a technology issue.

Cost: Free (some programs may have fees attached).

Application: Not applicable—information only.

Other Tips: If your company uses technology or creates a high-tech product, these offices can put you in touch with myriad state and local programs.

See below for individual state information.

STATE-BY-STATE SOURCES:
FUNDING FOR TECHNOLOGY-FOCUSED ORGANIZATIONS

ALABAMA—OFFICE FOR THE
   ADVANCEMENT OF DEVELOPING
   INDUSTRIES
University of Alabama at Birmingham
UAB Station
1075 13th St. S.
Birmingham, AL 35294
1-205-934-4011

ALASKA SCIENCE AND TECHNOLOGY
   FOUNDATION
4500 Diplomacy Drive, Suite 515
Anchorage, AK 99508-5918
1-907-272-4333

ARKANSAS SCIENCE AND TECHNOLOGY
    AUTHORITY
100 Main Street, Suite 450
Little Rock, AR 72201
1-501-324-9006

COLORADO—UNIVERSITY OF
    COLORADO BUSINESS
    ADVANCEMENT CENTERS
3333 Iris Avenue, Suite 101
Boulder, CO 80301
1-303-444-5723

CONNECTICUT INNOVATION INC.
40 Cold Springs Road
Rocky Hill, CT 06067
1-203-563-5851

FLORIDA—SOUTHERN TECHNOLOGY
    APPLICATIONS CENTER
One Progress Boulevard
Box 24
Alachua, FL 32615
1-800-225-0308
1-904-462-3913

GEORGIA—ADVANCED TECHNOLOGY
    DEVELOPMENT CENTER
430 Tenth Street, NW, Suite N-116
Atlanta, GA 30318
1-404-894-3575

HAWAII HIGH TECHNOLOGY
    DEVELOPMENT CORPORATION
300 Kahelu Avenue, Suite 35
Mililani, HI 96789
1-808-625-5293

INDIANA BUSINESS OF MODERNIZATION
    AND TECHNOLOGY CORPORATION
One North Capitol Avenue, Suite 925
Indianapolis, IN 46204
1-317-635-3058

IOWA—CENTER FOR INDUSTRIAL
    RESEARCH AND SERVICE
ISU Research Park, Suite 500
2501 North Loop Drive
Ames, IA 50010-8286
1-515-294-3420

KANSAS TECHNOLOGY ENTERPRISE
    CORPORATION
112 W. 6th Street, Suite 400
Topeka, KS 66603
1-913-296-5272

KENTUCKY BUSINESS & TECHNOLOGY
    BRANCH
Kentucky Cabinet for Economic
    Development
2400 Capitol Plaza Tower
500 Mero Street, 22nd Floor
Frankfort, KY 40601
1-502-564-7670

LOUISIANA BUSINESS AND
    TECHNOLOGY CENTER
South Stadium Drive
Louisiana State University
Baton Rouge, LA 70803-6100
1-504-334-5555

MAINE SCIENCE AND TECHNOLOGY
    FOUNDATION
87 Winthrop Street
Augusta, ME 04330
1-207-624-6350

MARYLAND—DEPARTMENT OF
    ECONOMIC AND EMPLOYMENT
    DEVELOPMENT
Division of Business Research
217 E. Redwood Street, 12th Floor
Baltimore, MD 21202
1-410-333-6990

MASSACHUSETTS TECHNOLOGY
DEVELOPMENT CORPORATION
148 State Street, 9th Floor
Boston, MA 02109
1-617-723-4920

MICHIGAN—BUSINESS RESOURCES
GROUP
P.O. Box 30225
Lansing, MI 48909
1-517-335-4720

MINNESOTA TECHNOLOGY, INC.
111 Third Avenue South, Suite 400
Minneapolis, MN 55401
1-612-338-7722

MISSISSIPPI ENTERPRISE FOR
TECHNOLOGY
John C. Stennis Space Center
Building 1103
Stennis Space Center, MS 39529-6000
1-601-688-3144

MONTANA SCIENCE AND TECHNOLOGY
ALLIANCE
46 N. Last Chance Gulch
Helena, MT 59601
1-406-449-2778

NEBRASKA SMALL BUSINESS
ADMINISTRATION
P.O. Box 8805-35
Lincoln, NE 68588-0535
1-402-221-4691

NEVADA—THE CENTER FOR BUSINESS
AND ECONOMIC RESEARCH AT THE
UNIVERSITY OF NEVADA LAS VEGAS
4505 South Maryland Parkway
P. O. Box 456002
Las Vegas, NV 89154
1-702-895-3191

NEW HAMPSHIRE—THE UNIVERSITY OF
NEW HAMPSHIRE
Vice President for Research and
Public Service
Room 113
108 Thompson Hall
Durham, NH 03824
1-603-862-1997

NEW JERSEY STATE COMMISSION ON
SCIENCE AND TECHNOLOGY
28 West State Street
CN 832
Trenton, NJ 08625
1-609-984-1671

NEW MEXICO—TECHNOLOGY
ENTERPRISE DIVISION
State of New Mexico Economic
Development Department
1009 Bradbury S.E.
Albuquerque, NM 87106
1-505-272-7576

NEW YORK STATE SCIENCE AND
TECHNOLOGY FOUNDATION
99 Washington Avenue, Suite 1730
Albany, NY 12210
1-518-474-4349

NORTH CAROLINA TECHNOLOGICAL
DEVELOPMENT AUTHORITY, INC.
2 Davis Drive
P.O. Box 13169
Research Triangle Park, NC 27709
1-919-990-8558

NORTH DAKOTA—CENTER FOR
INNOVATION AND BUSINESS
DEVELOPMENT
University of North Dakota
P.O. Box 8372
Grand Forks, ND 58202
1-701-777-3132

OHIO—THOMAS EDISON PROGRAM
77 S. High Street, 25th Floor
Columbus, OH 43266
1-614-466-3086

OKLAHOMA CENTER FOR THE
ADVANCEMENT OF SCIENCE AND
TECHNOLOGY
301 N.W. 63rd, Suite 110
Oklahoma City, OK 73116-7906
1-405-848-2633

OREGON RESOURCE AND TECHNOLOGY
DEVELOPMENT CORPORATION
1934 Broadway
Portland, OR 97232
1-503-282-4462

PENNSYLVANIA—OFFICE OF
TECHNOLOGY DEVELOPMENT
Pennsylvania Department of
Commerce
352 Forum Building
Harrisburg, PA 17120
1-717-787-4147

RHODE ISLAND PARTNERSHIP FOR
SCIENCE AND TECHNOLOGY
Rhode Island Department of
Economic Development
7 Jackson Walkway
Providence, RI 02903
1-401-277-2601

SOUTH CAROLINA—ENTERPRISE
DEVELOPMENT, INC. OF SOUTH
CAROLINA
P.O. Box 1149
1201 Main Street, Suite 2010
Columbia, SC 29202
1-803-737-0888

TENNESSEE TECHNOLOGY FOUNDATION
P.O. Box 23770
Knoxville, TN 37933-1170
1-615-694-6772

TEXAS—TECHNOLOGY BUSINESS
DEVELOPMENT
301 Tarrow Road
College Station, TX 77843-8000
1-409-845-2907

UTAH COMMUNITY AND ECONOMIC
PARTNERSHIPS
Weber State University
Ogden, UT 84408-4001
1-801-626-6344

VIRGINIA—CENTER FOR INNOVATIVE
TECHNOLOGY
CIT Tower
2214 Rock Hill Road, Suite 600
Herndon, VA 22070-4005
1-703-689-3000

WASHINGTON TECHNOLOGY CENTER
University of Washington
Sluke Hall, FJ-15
Seattle, WA 98195
1-206-685-1920

WEST VIRGINIA ROBERT C. BYRD
INSTITUTE FOR ADVANCED FLEXIBLE
MANUFACTURING SYSTEMS
1050 Fourth Avenue
Huntington, WV 25701
1-304-696-3092

UNIVERSITY OF WISCONSIN—MADISON
INDUSTRY RELATIONS
University of Wisconsin, Madison
1215 WARF Office Building
Room 1215
610 Walnut Street
Madison, WI 53705
1-608-263-2840

WYOMING—STATE/SCIENCE,
TECHNOLOGY AND ENERGY
AUTHORITY
c/o Terry Kling
P.O. Box 3295
Laramie, WY 82071
1-307-766-6797

5

Charge Cards

Selecting the right charge card(s) for your business isn't solely a matter of comparing interest rates cost and yearly fees. In fact, we suggest considering five criteria to determine which credit card(s) are best:

1. *Annual fees:* These days, fees range from free to $300 a year. If the card gives you services and privileges you can't get elsewhere, maybe the fee is worth it. If not, there are a number of no-fee cards. A tip: Some charge card companies will waive their fees if you call them and tell them you'll terminate unless they do so. This works better if you've made a lot of charges and always paid promptly.
2. *Interest rates:* What are they, and are they fixed or variable? At the time of this writing, interest rates are low. We suggest locking in a low-rate, fixed-rate card now. This is particularly important if you plan to carry a balance from month to month, or expect to have times during the year when you need to revolve.
3. *Service levels and ease of use:* Is it easy to dispute charges? To arrange for an on-the-spot credit limit increase? It's awfully inconvenient to be stuck somewhere waiting to have a charge approved, or wasting time trying to have a charge reversed.
4. *Special services or benefits:* Does your card offer frequent flyer miles? Discounts on goods and services? Cash rebates? Warranties or car rental insurance? End of year summaries of spending? Better cash flow? Some cards are designed to save your business money or make office administration easier.
5. *Billing cycles and interest policies.* Beware: Some cards bill on a 24-

day cycle, which shortens the time you get the use of money interest-free, reduces the time you have to pay the bill and increases the chance that you'll pay the bill late. Other cards (mostly from Texas banks) start assessing interest from the date of purchase, which means that you'll *always* pay an interest charge if you use the card.

If you haven't done so already, we suggest that you also explore the considerable benefits of charge cards designed specifically for small businesses. American Express and Diners Club both offer these types of cards. In addition, some banks offer Corporate Visa cards, although the level and type of benefits vary by bank.

American Express established its Small Business Services group first, and has captured the lion's share of small- and medium-sized businesses (they claim they serve over 1 million small businesses today). Diners Club has followed with a "me, too" product with similar benefits.

Just what are these benefits? They can be considerable, especially considering that the fee is relatively low and tax-deductible. For instance, the American Express Corporate Card provides:

- *Expense management:* Quarterly reports on spending, itemized by employee and by category of expenditure. And, of course, improved cash flow because you no longer need to "front" employees money for travel.
- *Disability insurance:* In case of accidental permanent and total disability, cardmembers get a lump sum payment ranging from $10–50,000 (the amount depends on the cardmember's tenure).
- *Buyer's Protection Plan* that extends the free repair period of many items (except motorized vehicles) for up to one year more than the original warranty.
- *Purchase Protection Plan* that protects you against theft or accidental damage of retail items for 90 days from purchase date.
- *Travel Benefits* including 10% off the standard corporate rate at a broad number of hotels, car rental insurance, lost/stolen/damaged baggage insurance, and worldwide 24-hour toll-free emergency assistance. Emergency assistance includes cash advances, emergency check cashing, rapid replacement of the card, and general assistance if you are ill, need help in setting up a business meeting abroad, or have issues or crises while travelling.

Another plus: if you have a personal American Express card, they'll also give you free enrollment in Membership Miles, where you accrue one mile for every dollar spent. (If you don't have another Amex card, you can join—but it costs you $50 per year.)

- *Purchasing Benefits* that provide 10% off AT&T long distance charges (if you spend at least $30 per quarter on AT&T Corporate Calling Card calls); up to 20% off standard leasing rates for most new domestic or imported cars, and extended payment terms with no finance charges for purchases of office equipment made through the American Express office equipment catalog.

Diners Club provides many similar benefits, but has some minuses (and some plusses, as well):

Minuses:

- No disability insurance
- No buying services
- Less acceptance worldwide: 2.3 million locations vs. Amex's 3.2 million

Plusses:

- Access to 48 business and airport lounges in foreign locations throughout the world
- Monthly spending reports (vs. quarterly for Amex)
- Higher automatic flight insurance: $350,000 vs. $100,000 for Amex
- *Two* points earned in their rewards program for every dollar spent.

Again, the choice is yours.

Corporate-based charge cards are definitely worth exploring, particularly if you do a lot of traveling or are having a hard time keeping up with expense paperwork. We provide telephone numbers in the Sources section that follows.

No matter what card you choose, there are a number of tips and tactics to help cut charge card costs:

- *Pay bills immediately if you're carrying a balance* or planning to do so. Charge card companies calculate your interest on "average daily balance," so reducing that balance as soon as possible will reduce your interest charges. (Note: If you're paying in full, of course, you'll want to wait until the last possible moment.)

- *Don't pay late*. Card companies charge significant penalties for late payment—and some, like the Optima Card, deny late payers access to the lowest possible interest rates.
- *Don't get more credit than you need*. You probably only need one or two cards; more can turn out to be an administrative headache and (if they're fee cards) a needless expense. Another, less obvious reason to cut down on cards: Banks tend to count your credit lines as a potential liability when determining whether to loan you money. Too many cards and too much credit makes lenders suspicious.

We can't tell you which cards are best for your business, but in the Sources section below we provide cards that seem to have advantages in at least one of the five criteria we list above—and a source for getting up-to-date information on what cards are offering the best credit-and-cost deals right now.

SOURCES:

CREDIT CARDS

Information About Credit Cards

Because bank card offers change every day, it's best to get up-to-date information on what's out there. Low-cost information sources include:

BANKCARD HOLDERS OF AMERICA
524 Branch Drive
Salem, VA 24153

1-703-389-5445

For $4, this nonprofit consumer credit education and advocacy organization will send you a list of 50 card companies that offer credit cards with low interest rates and no annual fee.

CARD TRAK
Box 1700
Frederick, MD 21702

1-301-695-4660

Card Trak is a monthly report listing 500 no-fee, low-interest Visa and MasterCard, including Gold Cards and Secured Cards. Each issue costs $5; to obtain, mail them a $5 check (be sure to include your return address!)

MONEY MAGAZINE
Time & Life Building
1271 Avenue of the Americas
New York, NY 10020

1-212-522-1212

Each month, this magazine features the lowest cost credit cards in a column, "Your Money Monitor." Newsstand price of "Money": $3.95.

Credit Cards to Consider

The right card for you depends on how you use it. Below, we offer a selection of cards with different benefits.

Lower-interest Cards, If You Carry a Balance:

AFBA Industrial Bank (MC/Visa; Standard)	1-800-776-2322
Arkansas Federal (MC/Visa; Standard and Gold)	1-800-477-3348
Central Carolina Bank of Georgia (MC/Visa; Standard)	1-800-577-1680
Federal Savings Bank (MC/Visa; Standard and Gold)	1-800-374-5600
Oak Brook Bank (MC; Gold)	1-800-536-3000

No-fee Cards, Lower-Interest Cards, If You Usually Pay in Full:

AFBA Industrial Bank (MC/Visa; Standard and Gold)	1-800-776-2322
Amalgamated Bank (MC; Standard and Gold)	1-800-723-0303
Oak Brook Bank (MC; Standard)	1-800-536-3000
USAA Federal Savings Bank (MC/Visa; Standard and Gold)	1-800-922-9092

Cards with Reputations for Extraordinary Service:

American Express	1-800-528-4800
AT&T Universal Card (MC/Visa)	1-800-662-7759
Citibank (MC/Visa; Standard and Gold)	1-800-456-4277

Cards with Special Services for Businesses:

American Express Corporate Card	1-800-528-2122
Diners Club Corporate Card	1-800-999-9093

Cards that Offer Rebates or Other Benefits:

FREQUENT FLYER/STAYER POINTS

Alaska Airlines (MC/Visa; Standard and Gold)	1-800-552-7302
America West Airlines (Visa; Standard)	1-800-243-7762

American Airlines/Citibank (MC/Visa; Standard)	1-800-359-4444
Best Western (MC, Standard)	1-800-668-0276
(For V, V Gold)	1-800-847-7378
Continental Airlines (MC/Visa; Standard and Gold)	1-800-446-5336
Northwest Airlines (Visa; Standard and Gold)	1-800-945-2004
Ramada Inns (MC; Standard and Gold)	1-800-672-6232
United Airlines (MC/Visa; Standard and Gold)	1-800-537-7783
(in Illinois only)	1-708-931-1450
USAir (Visa; Standard and Gold)	1-800-759-6262

REBATES/CASH BACK

Discover Card (Standard and Gold)	1-800-347-2683

6

Computer Software

Software expenses can really add up. Consider: The typical office usually needs a number of core software programs, including word-processing, spreadsheet, address/contact management and bookkeeping software. Other important applications include presentation, database and desktop publishing software and networking programs. You'll want programs that check diskettes for viruses, and applications that can help you quickly back up your hard drives. And you may need utility software to help you repair diskettes or retrieve data.

And these are just the basic needs. If you're like most people, you'll probably want to add some noncritical programs: clip art, games, labels, calendars, programs for your kids and whatever else strikes your fancy. The possibilities are endless—only your budget isn't. So you need ways to save on software. Some avenues for saving:

- *"Borrowing" software isn't good business.* First of all, as we all know, it's illegal. But even if you're not swayed by the ethical arguments, there are other good reasons to purchase, not steal, software. For instance, you'll spend much less time learning and using a software program if you have all the documentation and instructions that come with the purchased package. As a purchaser, you also have access to the help desk. And finally, you are eligible to receive upgrades at a fairly low cost, as soon as they're on the market—no more dependence on the kindness of your friends.
- *Buy from catalog houses.* There have been a proliferation of discount software catalog operations; for your convenience, we've selected ones

that have a track record and a broad product line. (Note: Even if you'd prefer the face-to-face interaction and "get it *now*" convenience of a local retail store, we suggest ordering a couple of catalogs in order to compare prices and see just what that convenience is costing you.)

If you buy via catalog houses, here are a couple of tips to help you garner additional savings:

- *Buy packages.* Several software companies have begun bundling some of their core software products together, resulting in big savings for you. For instance, at this writing, Microsoft OFFICE, containing Word, Excel, PowerPoint and Mail, is available for under $500; if purchased separately, these programs would cost well over $1,000. Microsoft, WordPerfect and Lotus all offer these bundles.
- *Check out package deals: hardware and software.* If you're also buying a computer, ask them if they'll bundle the cost of your software in with the hardware. Direct marketers of computers and peripherals who also carry software may do so. Another bonus: They'll often preload it for you, so you don't have to waste time loading it yourself.
- *Look for upgrades.* Once you buy the software, you can purchase upgrades at a substantial discount. Be sure to retain your documentation and send in your warranty card in order to be ready to take advantage of these offers.
- *Consider taking advantage of competitive upgrades.* Some software companies offer an incentive to users of the competition's software to switch to *their* software. Particularly if you're dissatisfied with your current programs, you may wish to "jump ship" at a discount.
- *Look for add-on specials.* Sometimes manufacturers or the catalog houses themselves will include additional software when you purchase a program.

- *Shareware is another excellent source of low-cost programs and games.* Shareware is a marketing and distribution concept that lets you "try before you buy" and brings you some great software for a very low price. For the cost of duplication and shipping you have 60–90 days to evaluate a working copy of a program. If you decide not to continue to use the program there is no further cost, and you can either reuse the disk or pass it along to a friend. If you wish to continue to use the program, you are expected to register with the author and pay a fee—generally, between $15 and $100. With registration, you get manuals, updates and technical support.

Programs cover the gamut of games, word processing, spreadsheets, page layout, educational programs and graphics. And there are cutting edge virtual reality and CD-ROM applications, at prices that are one-fifth to one-half of comparable commercial software. This is a great way to try a number of interesting and very useful pieces of software.

You can access shareware in a number of ways. First, if you're a member of either CompuServe or America Online, you can find many programs in the PC or Mac World Online Forum. You can also check out private bulletin board services, including:

Channel 1	1-617-354-8873
Exec-PC	1-414-789-4210
Executive Network	1-914-667-4567
HH Info-Net	1-203-738-0342

Even if you don't have a modem or you aren't a member of online services, you can still receive shareware, either through distributors or directly from the author. In the "Sources" section of this chapter, we provide information on some of the larger shareware distributors.

One important caveat if you're thinking of using shareware: *Be sure you have an up-to-date virus checker on your computer, and never, ever insert a shareware disk without checking it!* Although shareware companies guarantee that they'll check each disk, it's not worth taking a chance; you don't know where that disk has been.

• *Join a user group.* If you're a Macintosh owner, you should consider joining a user group. First, it's helpful to have access to people who also use Macintoshes and may have solutions to your problems. Second, user groups are great sources of shareware. Third, it gives you occasional access to highly discounted software, because software publishers often approach user groups, offering their newest products at substantial savings—up to half off—if the group can make a bulk purchase among its membership. Dues are reasonable, particularly considering the free or low-cost information and support you can access. To find out the phone number of the group nearest you, call the User Group Locator Number, 1-800-538-9696, Ext. 500.

On the following pages, we list some sources for shareware and discount software.

SOURCES:

SOFTWARE

EDUCORP
7434 Trade Street
San Diego, CA 92121-2410

1-800-843-9497 (orders)
1-619-536-9999 (information and technical support)

Educorp provides shareware and interactive media for Macintosh computers. They have a great selection of "almost free" software—lots of clip art
and other programs for as low as $3.99 per diskette. And they will meet or
beat any advertised price on CD-ROM products.

Outlet Type:	Catalog house.
Product Line:	For Macintosh only: Shareware, CD-ROM drives, interactive media/CD-ROM titles.
Fax:	1-619-536-2345
Information:	Catalog, or call info number above. Technical support available: call 1-619-536-9999, ext. 5.
Orders Accepted By:	Phone, fax, mail.
Payment:	MasterCard, Visa, American Express, Discover, personal or corporate check, money order.
Delivery:	UPS ground; $4.75 charge. Fed Ex available for $4 extra.
Guarantees:	Exchange only; defective and incompatible shareware disks will be replaced with other disks; a 25% restocking fee may apply to returned nonshareware items in saleable condition.

EGGHEAD SOFTWARE
22011 S.E. 51st Street
P.O. Box 7007
Issaquah, WA 98027-7007

1-800-EGGHEAD (1-800-344-4323)
1-206-391-0800 (corporate offices)
1-800-949-3447 (TDD)

Egghead is a national retailer that offers good discounts on PC- and Mac-based products. They also have a catalog operation, so you can access them even if you aren't close to one of their outlets. Our suggestion: Become a "CUE" member ("CUE" stands for "Custom Updates and 'Eggstras' "). Joining is free and you'll save 5% on everyday pricing and receive special offers and upgrades every 4–6 weeks.

Outlet Type:	Discount retailer, catalog house.
Product Line:	Full line of Macintosh and PC software; peripherals, hardware, and accessories.
Fax:	1-206-391-6200
Information:	Catalog; in store. No technical support available.
Orders Accepted By:	Phone, fax, mail, in store.
Payment:	MasterCard, Visa, American Express, Discover, check or money order. Qualified firms can also open an account.
Delivery:	Airborne overnight ($10) and UPS ground service ($5).
Guarantees:	30-day money-back guarantee if goods are returned unopened. If opened, defective merchandise can be exchanged for new merchandise. Manufacturers' warranties are also honored.

MAC WAREHOUSE/MICRO WAREHOUSE (PC)

P.O. Box 3013
1720 Oak Street
Lakewood, NJ 08701-3013

1-800-367-7080 (PC)
1-800-255-6227 (MacIntosh)

Via two different catalogs, Mac/Micro Warehouse caters to the entire PC/
Macintosh world. Not only do they offer an extremely broad line of software applications and good prices on upgrades, but they also carry utilities,
accessories and a good selection of peripherals.

Outlet Type:	Catalog house.
Product Line:	Broad line of software for Macintosh (through Mac Warehouse) DOS, Windows, and OS2 platforms (through Micro Warehouse). Good selection of hardware (monitors, printers, scanners, drives, speakers and CD-ROM drives) and accessories.
Fax:	1-908-370-2437 (Macintosh) 1-908-363-4834 (Macintosh upgrades) 1-908-905-5245 (PC)
Information:	Catalog. Technical support available Monday–Friday 9 AM–midnight; Saturday 9–6 Eastern Standard Time.
Orders Accepted By:	Phone, fax, mail.
Payment:	MasterCard, Visa, Discover, American Express, check or money order; COD with additional $7 charge; qualified firms may open a corporate account.
Delivery:	Shipped via UPS ground service; Airborne overnight available at additional charge; orders received by midnight will be received next day.
Guarantees:	Many programs come with a 30-day money-back guarantee; MW also offers a 120-day warranty against defects. Customer pays return shipping and handling unless program is defective.

PC CONNECTION/MAC CONNECTION
6 Mill Street
Marlow, NH 03456

1-800-800-5555 (PC)
1-800-800-2222 (Macintosh)

A broad line supplier of software, a little lighter on peripherals than some of the other suppliers. However, we love the notion of being able to order something by 3:15 AM and get it the same day.

Outlet Type:	Catalog house.
Product Line:	Full-line software supplier, offering applications compatible with Macintosh, DOS, Windows, and OS/2 platforms. Moderate line of peripherals. Toll-free tech support available on all products.
Fax:	1-603-446-7791
Information:	Catalog, MacTV™ for Macintosh-compatible product demos (call 1-800-800-6912 for information on MacTV).
Orders Accepted By:	Phone, fax, mail.
Payment:	MasterCard, Visa, American Express; check with order; COD (additional $4.50 charge, maximum $1,000 order with corporate check); qualified firms may set up corporate accounts.
Delivery:	Airborne overnight except when within UPS 1-day ground service. Cost: $5 for PC items; $3 for Macintosh items. (Items ordered midnight–3:15 AM will arrive that same day.) Weekend shipment; Saturday delivery available at no extra charge in many areas.
Guarantees:	Money-back guarantees on most products. 120-day minimum warranty on all products.

PC Zone/Mac Zone
17411 NE Union Hill Road
Redmond, WA 98052

1-800-258-2088 (PC)
1-800-248-0800 (Macintosh)

Good prices, great selection on full line of software and peripherals. PC users should ask for the PC Zone catalog; Macintosh users for the Mac Zone catalog.

Outlet Type:	Catalog house.
Product Line:	Full-line supplier of PC, Windows, OS2 software (under "PC Zone" name) and Macintosh applications (under "Mac Zone" name). Good selection of peripherals, too. They offer tech support, too: for Macintosh, 8 AM–6 PM Monday–Friday, Pacific Standard Time; for PCs, 7 AM–6 PM
Fax:	1-206-861-6663 (PC) 1-206-881-3421 (Mac)
Information:	Catalog.
Orders Accepted By:	Phone, fax, mail.
Payment:	MasterCard, Visa, American Express, Discover, check by mail.
Delivery:	Overnight by Airborne (approximately $6) except when within UPS 1-day ground service ($3).
Guarantees:	30-day limited warranty. (May differ, depending on manufacturers' warranties—check when you order.)

Reasonable Solutions
1221 Disk Drive
Medford, OR 97501-6639

1-800-876-3475
1-503-776-5777 (technical support)

Reasonable Solutions provides over 400 shareware titles for IBM PCs and compatibles, including many exclusives. They also provide a lot of technical support, and in-depth support is provided by the individual program authors. Finally, they will beat any nationally advertised price on shareware that they carry.

Outlet Type: Catalog house.

Product Line: Broad line of shareware for PC–compatible computers. Excellent support, including access to actual shareware authors; call 1–503–776–5777 8 AM–4 PM, M–F, Pacific Standard Time.

Fax: 1–503–773–7803

Information: Catalog.

Orders Accepted By: Phone, fax, mail.

Payment: MasterCard, Visa, Discover, check, money order, COD at $5 additional charge.

Delivery: $4 shipping and handling (by 1st class mail); Fed Ex next day (add $7); Fed Ex 2nd day (add $5).

Guarantees: Lifetime exchange or credit if disks are not compatible with your system or are defective.

ROCKY MOUNTAIN COMPUTER OUTFITTERS

P.O. Box 7850
Kalispell, MT 59904-0850

1-800-814-0009

Computer Outfitters prides itself on training its sales consultants on the products they carry, so that they can help you decide what you'll need and whether it will be compatible with your equipment. They carry software and peripherals for both Macintoshes and PCs, and they really care about getting the right merchandise for you.

Outlet Type: Catalog house.

Product Line: Mac and PC software; Mac and PC peripherals, including CD-ROM drives, external Mac drives, scanners, batteries, floppies and much more. They offer tech support, Monday–Friday, 8 AM–7 PM Rocky Mountain Time. Sales consultants can assist you with compatibility questions.

Fax: 1-800-895-0009

Information: Catalog.

**Orders Accepted
By:**   Phone, fax, mail. If you use fax or mail, they recommend calling before placing your order to check compatibility—especially if you own a PC.

Payment: MasterCard, Visa, American Express, Discover, check and wire transfers.

Delivery: Overnight by Airborne except when within UPS 1-day ground service. Flat cost: $3.

Guarantees: Any unopened merchandise can be returned for money back within 30 days. You must pay return shipping. If product is defective and needs to be replaced, they will pay for shipping. Other warranties are based on what the manufacturer offers; check with sales consultant before ordering to confirm warranty.

The Software Labs

8700 148th Avenue, N.E.
Redmond, WA 98052

1-800-569-7900

The Software Labs provides a variety of business and personal shareware applications for PC-based platforms, including Windows and OS/2. We particularly like their selection of Virtual Reality and games and entertainment products. However, at this writing they're a little light on business applications.

Outlet Type: Catalog house.

Product Line: For PC-based platforms, shareware in a wide range of subjects: entertainment, music, spreadsheets,

even religion and astrology. An issue: They offer
only limited tech support hours. For help call
1-206-869-6729 2–4 PM, M–F, Pacific Standard
Time.

Fax:	1-206-869-1500
Information:	Catalog.
Orders Accepted By:	Phone, fax, mail.
Payment:	MasterCard, Visa, check, money order.
Delivery:	UPS ground service or U.S. mail ($4); next day air (add $12); 2nd day air (add $5).
Guarantees:	Will replace any disk that is unreadable or improperly labeled.

TIGER SOFTWARE

One Datron Center
Suite 1200
9100 South Dadeland Boulevard
Miami, FL 33156

1-800-666-2562 (Macintosh)
1-800-888-4437 (PC/DOS)

Tiger offers a full line of software for Macs and PCs. You might check out
their "Tiger Gold Club"—for a $50 fee you get special discounts and offers
that vary each month (sometimes it's 10% off your order). If you're not
happy within six months, they'll refund your fee.

Outlet Type:	Catalog house.
Product Line:	Complete software supplier. They have Macintosh, DOS, Windows and OS/2 platforms as well as some very interesting peripherals, printers and even a few computers. They do not offer tech support.
Fax:	1-305-447-0738
Information:	Catalog.

**Orders Accepted
By:**   Phone, fax, mail.

Payment: MasterCard, Visa, American Express, Discover,
                           Diners Club, personal or business checks with
                           order.

Delivery: Fed Ex 2-day based on weight and dollar amount
                           of order. Overnight service available at extra
                           charge. UPS also available.

Guarantees: 30-day guarantee for replacement or Tiger credit;
                           money back if software is unopened.

7

Computers and Peripherals

Wisely selecting and purchasing your business's computers is a critical task, not only because of the significant initial cash outlay, but also because of the impact it will have on your business operations and capabilities.

Before you read any further, we have to explain that the "platform" you choose—PC or Macintosh—really affects the purchasing process. If you choose a Macintosh system, bear in mind that:

- You won't save as much money with a Macintosh. Macintosh prices are generally higher than PCs for the same computing power. They have other benefits, of course—we personally love them, and used them to put together this book. But there's no way around it: The upfront out-of-pocket costs *are* higher.
- There are no "national" mail-order suppliers of Apple computers, because Apple won't allow its authorized dealers to sell outside their prescribed geographic territories. (We expect this to change sometime in 1995, when the PowerPC is fully established and Apple realigns its distribution system to more closely match the PC distribution system.)

The combination of non-national distribution and almost-parity pricing means we've found it difficult to include Macintosh computer sources in this book for new computers. Don't despair if you're a confirmed Mac lover: Later in this text, we'll tell you how you can save thousands on Macintoshes in the aftermarket. And of course, we've been able to include Macintosh-compatible peripheral suppliers.

All that won't help you if you're in the market for a new, lowest-cost Mac, however. So here are some suggestions to help ensure you get a good deal and don't spend too much time shopping:

1. Start by shopping at a national chain, such as CompUSA, Nobody Beats The Wiz, Circuit City and the like. Their prices are generally competitive, if not rock bottom. You can get a good sense of the market.
2. Read the newspapers to find other Macintosh suppliers. These will include both retailers and regional telemarketing operations. Call them and see if they'll beat the national competitors' prices. Sometimes, their overhead is lower and they'll "deal"—particularly on larger orders.

Now, if you're a PC user, finding a good discount source is not difficult. We've been able to include a number of them in the Sources section, below. The hard part will be threading your way through the maze of competitive offerings. Another issue will be adding peripherals after your initial purchase, because the plethora of manufacturers and products out there often creates compatibility problems. If you're using a PC platform, make sure your peripheral supplier offers good tech support!

Whether you're buying a PC or a Mac, there are a number of things you can do to ensure that you get the computer you need at a fair price.

- *Determine the product features you want.* Particularly if you're buying via direct mail, you'll find it much easier to shop if you've determined what you're looking for. You will have to resolve a number of questions:

  - How *easy should it be* to operate?
  - How much *power and speed* do you need—now and later?
  - What *critical functions* do you particularly need it to do well?
  - What *other functions* do you need it to be capable of performing?
  - What *external peripherals* will you need—now and later?
  - What *user features* do you need, e.g., portability, screen size, etc.?

  You can answer these questions by talking to experts, reading magazines or joining a users' group, as well as by examining your business and the type of computer resources it needs. One tip: Always try to buy more than you think you need, especially when it comes to memory-related items like hard drives, RAM (random access memory) and video memory or VRAM. Memory is relatively cheap—and there's nothing more frustrating than not having enough of it.

- *Once you know what you need, make a list of the features you want.* Then shop around, using the list as a way to compare "apples to apples"—no pun intended. (Remember: If you've decided on a Macintosh, bear in mind that most Macs come without monitor, keyboard, mouse and modem. These should appear on your list as separate items.) To help you get started, below is the feature list we developed to comparison shop for IBM and IBM-clone PCs for this book. (Don't expect every supplier to be able to match your list exactly—you'll have to fudge a little.):

PC Feature List	Example
Processor:	486 DX 33Mhz
Case:	Standard
Operating system:	MS-DOS 6 (loaded), Windows .3.1
Internal memory (RAM):	8 Meg (upgradable to 32 Meg)
Video ram (VRAM):	1 Meg (local bus)
Disk cache:	256K
I/O ports:	2 Serial/1 Parallel
Floppy drives:	1–3.5" 1.44K
Hard drive:	230 Meg IDE
CD-ROM:	NEC dual speed
Expandable slots:	5 slots 3–16 bit half slots/2 –32 bit full VESA
FAX/modem:	Hayes compatible 14,400 Baud
Keyboard:	101 key with numerical keypad
Pointer:	Microsoft Mouse (not just Microsoft compatible)
Monitor:	14" Interlaced SVGA/.28 pitch
Power:	200 Watts

- *Think through your peripheral needs—now and in the future.* What peripherals—networking products, multimedia boards, modems, video products, CD-ROM drives, etc.—do you think you're going to need? The nice thing is that you can add peripherals on at anytime—but your computer has to be powerful enough to run them, and have the physical capacity to accommodate them.
- *Pick your retail channel.* Once you know what you're looking for, you

can decide what channel you're going to purchase through: direct mail or retailer. Each has its benefits and drawbacks.

- Purchasing from a *direct mail catalog* certainly is convenient: Just pick up the phone, send your fax or even modem your order in, then wait for delivery in a couple of days. These suppliers often offer the lowest prices, too. However, you may feel wary of ordering from an organization you don't know and from a person you've never seen. And you may feel that if anything goes wrong, it can be a hassle to get service. Our view: Direct mail is better for more experienced computer users and purchasers. New users probably need the sales and service support of retailers—but call a couple direct mail companies and see how you feel.

- *Retailers, specifically computer superstores,* put you face-to-face with a sales person. Moreover, they offer full-line selection, one-stop shopping, great discounts and lots of service. You get to see and try the product before you buy, and often you can walk out the same day with the products you want. But they can be slightly more expensive than mail order, and it can be harder to put together some of the more "estoric" custom configurations. They tend to carry more "ready-made" systems.

- *Don't forget the aftermarket.* Can you still work effectively with high-quality, but less "cutting-edge" computers? If so, consider the aftermarket, which sells used and new-but-outdated computers at substantial discounts. The key thing to remember is that many "outdated" models are perfect for a small business's needs. For instance, Apple introduced the Performa 450 in April 1993 at a list price of $1700 and replaced it with a slightly faster Performa 475 a couple months later. Result: In December, 1993, the 450 could be bought, new, for $800 on the aftermarket—a savings of 53%—and the 450 was covered by the standard Apple 90-day warranty.

Macintosh owners have two excellent ways to access the aftermarket: via specialized auctioneers and brokers, and through Macintosh User Groups. Auctioneers are authorized to sell off excess inventory, and if a sale is taking place near your city, you can really get a great bargain. Note that PCs are also often available for auction. (See "Ross-Dove" in the "Sources—Computers" section for more information; Ross-Dove is the Apple-authorized auctioneer for Macintoshes.)

User groups are also a very powerful resource for "aftermarket" sales. Through an umbrella group set up by Apple, User Group Connection (formerly Apple Computer department), user group members can purchase from a limited selection of refurbished Apple computers and peripherals. These are models that have recently left the official price list, and were returned either by dealers or endusers. The selection changes monthly, depending on what the User Group Connection can arrange with Apple. To join a Mac User Group near you, call the User Group Locator Number, 1-800-538-9696, Ext. 500.

Both Macintosh and PC users can access used computers through the various "computer exchanges"—brokerages that deal in used, new-but-discontinued, refurbished, trade-in, demo and "as-is" computers. These brokerages put buyers and sellers together, taking a commission on the transaction. If you don't need a cutting-edge computer—just solid computing power—you can save 20–40% and more off original prices. Note, however, that most exchanges don't offer much in the way of warranties and tech support. (However, if you buy factory refurbished equipment, which many exchanges *do* sell, you'll get manufacturer's warranties and tech support.) Another drawback: Many of the older used models on the market can't support Windows or Mac's System 7—which reduces your flexibility in adding peripherals and using some software. We've included several computer exchanges in the Sources section, below.

Whatever channel you ultimately use, here are some tips to buy smarter and make the process less painful.

If you're ordering by direct mail:

- *Get several suppliers' catalogs/quotes and compare.* Prices vary significantly. It makes sense to comparison shop.
- *Always confirm what you're ordering—in writing!* There are so many possible configurations and products that it's very easy to get confused. You'll wind up with something you don't want, and it can be a hassle to return it.
- *Ask if the computer will come ready to plug in and run.* This is particularly important if you're ordering an IBM/IBM clone, as setting up hardware for a PC can get pretty hairy. You can save a lot of time and avoid possible service calls by having experienced technicians do your work before they ship it.
- *Check out package deals: hardware and software.* Many direct marketers of computers also carry software, and some will negotiate a package price that includes the software you need. Another bonus: They'll

often preload it for you, so you don't have to waste time loading it yourself.

- *Always get a written quote for the system.* Have the supplier mail or fax a copy of the quote. You'll be able to compare systems more carefully and ensure you're getting what you think you're getting. Ultimately, you might be able to use these quotes to negotiate a better price.
- *Ask for unadvertised specials.* Sometimes, the best buys don't make it into the catalog or circular. It never hurts to ask!
- *Check their guarantees.* Make sure they offer a money-back guarantee whereby they refund the purchase price if you're not satisfied with the merchandise. Check to see whether the guarantee extends to their paying the return freight. And see if they offer a "lowest price" guarantee where they'll refund the difference between their price and a lower-priced competitor. (Sometimes, they'll even add a further discount on the price!)
- *Negotiate volume discounts.* If you need more than one computer, don't be shy about asking them to give you a price break. Use your buying power.

If you're purchasing in a store:

- *Use the information in catalogs to negotiate with local suppliers.* Before paying their asking prices, ask local suppliers if they can approach or match catalogers' prices. You can often negotiate good discounts, while still receiving same day delivery and dealing face-to-face with a real person.
- *Befriend the store manager, and let him or her know your needs.* Not only will you get better service, but you also might get first dibs on returns, items that are going on sale because a newer model is coming and get "freebies" thrown in.
- *Look for unadvertised specials.* Stop by occasionally to see what's on sale. Often, stores have sales when a new model is waiting in the wings—so when you hear that the "next generation" of computers has arrived, be aware that the current generation may be available at substantial savings.
- *Negotiate volume discounts.* If you need more than one computer, don't be shy about asking the manager to give you a price break. He or she wants to move the goods.
- *Buy from circulars.* These stores feature their loss-leaders in their promotional pieces. Read them and save.

SOURCES:

COMPUTERS AND PERIPHERALS

The pages that follow provide sources for PCs and Macintosh computers and peripherals. Although we've included a lot of suppliers, there are so many out there that we couldn't include them all. To make it more manageable for you, we've done some fairly rigorous screening, using the following criteria:

- *Discounting policy*. Although they may not always offer the lowest price on every single item, they have to be competitive.
- *Service support*. Do they offer an 800 number for service? Is it accessible, and open long hours? For how long do they offer free support?
- *Guarantees*. The company must offer a liberal return policy and provide a satisfaction guarantee.
- *Longevity*. You'd be unhappy if, six months down the road, you called your supplier with a question and got, "Sorry, that number has been disconnected." We've included suppliers with a track record.
- *Product quality*. This applies to PCs, not Macintoshes. We've tried to pick PC manufacturer/wholesalers with reputations for excellent quality.

ACER AMERICA CORP.
2641 Orchard Parkway
San Jose, CA 95134

1-800-848-ACER (1-800-848-2237)

Acer claims to be the largest OEM (original equipment manufacturer) supplier of PCs and has been in business for 18 years. They claim that the biggest and the best computer companies buy Acer's "guts" and put their own names on them. Acer is a top-to-bottom source for computer hardware and can configure a system to your specifications.

Outlet Type:	Manufacturer.
Product Line:	Full line of PCs and notebooks, plus some peripherals.
Fax:	1-408-922-2953
Information:	Catalog (free).
Orders Accepted By:	Phone, mail, fax, computer modem (PC only).
Payment:	Visa, MasterCard, American Express.
Lease:	Available.
Technical Support:	24 hours/7 days a week toll free.
Delivery:	UPS 2-day service. Fed Ex next day (extra charge).
Guarantees:	Money back within 30 days if not satisfied. Replacement parts within 72 hours.
On-Site Service:	On desktop systems, service provided within 48 hours for one year. On notebooks there is no need for on-site service; they'll just get you a replacement within 24 hours.

AMBRA, AN IBM SUBSIDIARY

3200 Beachleaf Court
Raleigh, NC 27614
Mailing address for orders:
P.O. Box 101790
Atlanta, GA 30392-1790

1-800-25-AMBRA (1-800-252-6272)
1-800-363-0066, Ext. 910 (in Canada)

IBM has paired up with Insight as their marketing partner in order to compete in the "clone" market, creating AMBRA. Just try to imagine a PC clone made by IBM and you have an AMBRA: a good performer, built to IBM's quality specs. AMBRA is very price competitive and offers the kind of service and technical know-how you'd expect from IBM. All AMBRA systems are custom-built and turnaround time from receipt of order is usually 6–8 days. Machines all come standard with the current versions of DOS and Windows loaded.

Outlet Type:	Manufacturer.
Product Line:	Full line of PCs and notebooks, plus some peripherals.
Fax:	1-602-858-2630
Information:	Catalog (free).
Orders Accepted By:	Phone, mail, fax.
Payment:	Cash, check, money order, MasterCard, Visa, Discover.
Lease Terms:	Available. Call for details.
Technical Support:	24 hours/7 days a week.
Delivery:	Fed Ex 2nd day service.
Store Locations:	None.
Guarantees:	Returns accepted within 30 days or exchange, refund or credit.
On-Site Service:	3-year service; maximum charge $29; service provided within 6–8 days.

AMERICAN COMPUTER EXCHANGE

6065 Roswell Road
Suite 535
Atlanta, GA 30328

1-800-786-0717

American Computer Exchange, like other computer exchanges, allows you access to used, refurbished, new-but-discontinued, "as-is," liquidated, trade-in and demo computers—all at substantial savings of 20% or more. You call and tell them what you're looking for. They check their databases and come back with a seller and a price. It's that simple.

Outlet Type:　　　Computer exchange.

Product Line:　　New-and-discontinued, refurbished, returned, used and demo models of computers from all major manufacturers, including PCs and Apples.

Fax:　　　　　　1-404-250-1399

Information:　　　Phone.

**Orders Accepted
By:**　　　　　　　Phone, fax.

Payment:　　　　Deposits must be paid by check, wire transfer, or money order. Balance paid COD when computer is delivered.

Delivery:　　　　Seller and buyer arrange delivery.

**Technical
Support:**　　　　　Manufacturer's tech support on refurbished equipment. Otherwise, no tech support.

Guarantees:　　　Manufacturer's warranty on refurbished equipment. All equipment is guaranteed operational, with money back or replacement.

AUSTIN, AN IPC COMPANY

10300 Metric Boulevard
Austin, TX 78758

1-800-483-9938

Austin has been in business for eight years and has a reputation for one of the fastest response times in tech service (75 seconds). They are owned by the Singapore giant IPC, so they're likely to stick around.

Outlet Type:　　　Manufacturer.

Product Line:　　Full line of PCs and notebooks, plus some peripherals.

Fax:　　　　　　1-512-454-1357

Information:　　　Catalog (free).

**Orders Accepted
By:**   Phone, mail, fax.

Payment: Cash, check, Visa, MasterCard, American Express.

Lease Terms: Available; call for details.

**Technical
Support:**   6 AM to midnight, 7 days a week, with an average
                               response time of 75 seconds.

Delivery: UPS 2-day ground service in Texas. Fed Ex
                               everywhere else with no charge for notebooks.
                               Desktops are assessed a freight but you should
                               check in advance what it will be; each system is a
                               little different.

Guarantees: Money back within 30 days if not satisfied.

On-Site Service: The first year is free and you can purchase up to a
                               total of 3 years of on-site service.

BOSTON COMPUTER EXCHANGE

55 Temple Place
Boston, MA 02111

1-800-262-6399
1-617-542-4414

Boston Computer is a computer exchange that sells new-disconinued, used and return/demo PCs and Apples at deep discount. They participate in the trade-in programs for companies like Hewlitt-Packard and Toshiba, so they have excellent supplies of a broad variety of these computers, as well as a broad line of other "major manufacturer" computers. Their selection varies daily, so even if they don't have exactly what you want one day, they will the next.

Outlet Type: Computer exchange.

Product Line: New-and-discontinued, returned, used, and demo
                               models of computers from major manufacturers:
                               IBM, Toshiba, Hewlitt-Packard, Compaq, NEC
                               and Apple. Selection varies, but ranges from 286 to
                               Pentiums.

Fax:	1-617-542-8849
Information:	Phone.
Orders Accepted By:	Phone, fax.
Payment:	MasterCard, Visa, check, COD, corporate accounts.
Delivery:	UPS ground service, at customer's expense. Overnight delivery available.
Technical Support:	No formal tech support, but personnel will answer questions.
Guarantees:	30-day parts and labor; 7-day return for money back.

COMPAQ DIRECT PLUS

P.O. Box 692025
Houston, TX 77269-2025

1-800-888-5886

Compaq has long been considered one of the most successful manufacturers of high quality PCs. Although they have tended to cost more than the other vendors, you always got a solid product and good service. Now that competition is so fierce in the PC market, some of their basic computers have come down in price.

Outlet Type:	Manufacturer.
Product Line:	Complete line of computers, including notebooks.
Fax:	1-800-888-5329
Information:	Catalog (free).
Orders Accepted By:	Phone, fax.
Payment:	Check or money order, corporate account, Visa, MasterCard, Discover, American Express.

Lease Terms:	Yes, 36 month by GE Capital Services.
Technical Support:	24 hours a day, 7 days a week.
Delivery:	2nd day air is normal, but they can ship next day.
Guarantees:	30-day money back guarantee.
On-Site Service:	Yes. Cost per PC is either $165 for Deluxe Care or $195 for Ultimate Care.

COMPUADD COMPUTER CORPORATION

12303 Technology Boulevard
Austin, Texas 78727

1-800-626-1967

Compuadd is one of the biggest suppliers of PCs in the world. One reason is that they buy everything in bulk, so they can pass the savings on to you. In fact, they have some of the lowest prices to be found on computers, peripherals and some software.

Outlet Type:	Manufacturer.
Product Line:	Full line of PCs and notebooks, plus some peripherals and software.
Fax:	1-512-250-1489
Information:	Catalog (free).
Orders Accepted By:	Phone, mail, fax.
Payment:	Cash, check, Visa, MasterCard, American Express.
Lease Terms:	Available through Bell Atlantic.
Technical Support:	Toll free Monday–Saturday: 7 AM–12 PM
Delivery:	UPS. (An example: We were quoted $38.73 on our sample system.) Overnight and 2nd day air are available at extra charge.
Guarantees:	Money back within 30 days if not satisfied. 1 year warranty on parts and labor.

On-Site Service: Most systems include on-site service, but check on the system you order.

COMPUDYNE/COMPUSA DIRECT

15167 Business Avenue
Dallas, TX 75244

1-800-COMPUSA

Compudyne is a catalog house; CompUSA is a computer superstore. They are the same company. Both offer broad product lines and excellent prices. Their support lines are open 24 hours a day, seven days a week, and they'll come on-site to fix a problem if it can't be resolved over the phone.

Outlet Type: Manufacturer, superstore.

Product Line: Various 486s, Pentiums and Notebooks, peripherals, software, accessories.

Fax: 1-800-FAX-2212

Information: Catalog (free).

Orders Accepted By: Phone, mail, fax; in-store.

Payment: Cash, check, Visa, MasterCard, Discover.

Lease Terms: Various leases available.

Technical Support: 24 hours, 7 days a week.

Delivery: UPS 2-day ground service. Next day Fed Ex available at extra charge.

Guarantees: Money back within 30 days if not satisfied.

On-Site Service: Next day on-site service if problem can't be solved over the phone.

COMPUTABILITY CONSUMER ELECTRONICS

P.O. Box 17882
Milwaukee, WI 53217

1-800-554-9930

One of the largest and most reliable sources of peripherals, CCE has been in business for 12 years and prides themselves on the quality of their products and service. A plus: They don't sell refurbished goods—only brand new equipment. Nor do they sell OEM versions—only brand names here, with pretty good prices and reliable service.

Outlet Type:	Catalog house.
Product Line:	Complete peripheral products; a full selection of software, some laptops and PCs.
Fax:	1-800-554-9981
Information:	Catalog.
Orders Accepted By:	Phone, fax, mail.
Payment:	MasterCard, Visa, check, COD with $6 surcharge.
Delivery:	UPS. Hardware 5% of order or $5 min. On software, there is a $6 shipping charge per order (not per title).
Technical Support:	Call 1-414-357-8181 Monday–Friday: 1–5 PM Central Time.
Guarantees:	30-day limited warranty. 5% restocking fee charged, however.

COMPUTER DISCOUNT WAREHOUSE
1020 East Lake Cook Road
Buffalo Grove, IL 60089

1-800-349-4CDW (1-800-349-4239)

Although CDW is primarily a peripheral and computer accessories house, they also sell a limited line of Apples and PCs. Although currently, Apple won't allow them to sell outside of their local area (Chicago), CDW says that they will be one of first catalog houses to sell Apples nationally when Apple permits this (probably starting in 1995).

Outlet Type:	Catalog house, with one store at 315 West Grand, Chicago, IL.

Product Line:	Complete line of peripheral products. Also has a limited line of computers and laptops.
Fax:	1-708-465-6800
Information:	Catalog.
Orders Accepted By:	Phone, mail, fax.
Payment:	MasterCard, Visa, American Express, Discover, check 12 working days (must clear in advance). COD, certified money order, cashiers check; if UPS, they'll take cash, too.
Delivery:	UPS. Special: overnight by UPS to the western half of the U.S. for the same price as UPS ground service.
Technical Support:	Monday–Friday: 9 AM–7 PM.
Guarantees:	Money back if returned within 15 days.

DC DRIVES
1110 Nasa Road One, Suite 304
Houston, TX 77058

1-800-473-0962

Although DC Drives specializes in storage devices (drives) they also stock and sell a very broad array of peripherals. Because they specialize, their prices are very competitive—often lower than other suppliers. We bought our Syquest drive here and received it the next day. Plus, we had an installation question and the tech support was fast and accurate.

Outlet Type:	Catalog house.
Product Line:	Specializes in drives: hard, floppies and flopticals, removable, tape backup and more. They also carry other peripherals—mostly data storage peripherals. They also carry a full line of CD-ROM drives.
Fax:	1-713-333-3024

Information:	Catalog.
Offers Accepted By:	Phone, fax, mail.
Payment:	MasterCard, Visa, American Express, Discover, check.
Delivery:	Fed Ex, 90% shipped the same day the order is placed.
Technical Support:	Call 1-713-333-2099, Monday–Friday: 9 AM–6 PM
Guarantees:	30-day limited warranty.

DELL USA L.P.

9505 Arboretum Boulevard
Austin, Tx 78759-7299

1-800-727-3355

Dell has long been a leader in the computer industry. They claim that, because they use the highest quality materials, a Dell computer will outperform a similarly configured competitor. Dell puts out one of the most informative catalogs, and offers a full line of IBM/IBM clones, including notebooks. They also offer software. A big plus: They guarantee your Dell computer will run any and all software now available or that becomes available for the next three years. Another plus: fast delivery on custom orders— they can ship it to you by overnight express. Tip: They also run special promotions, so ask for the specials that day.

Outlet Type:	Manufacturer.
Product Line:	Complete line of PC clones and notebooks, printers, software.
Fax:	1-800-727-8320
Information:	Catalog (free).
Orders Accepted By:	Phone, mail, fax.
Payment:	Checks, money order, Visa, MasterCard, Discover, American Express.

Lease Terms: Available—call for details.

**Technical
Support:**   24 hours a day, 7 days a week, toll free.

Delivery: They prefer to send it via Airborne
                          overnight—but there is a charge. If you prefer,
                          request UPS ground service, which is generally less
                          expensive, but slower.

Guarantees: Money back within 30 days. Also have a 3-year
                          software compatibility warranty.

On-Site Service: Yes, if they can't solve the problem over the
                          phone.

GATEWAY 2000

610 Gateway Drive/P.O. Box 2000
North Sioux City, SD 57049-2000

1-800-846-2000
1-605-232-2000 (local)

Gateway is so big, they even have an office in Tallinn, Estonia! Gateway
keeps their prices down by cutting their overhead and buying in volume.
For instance, they say they operate out of a "tin shack" in South Dakota—
they claim their buying power allows them to undersell any vendor. All
machines are custom configured on a first-in, first-out inventory basis. And
a big plus: Gateway offers free technical support.

Outlet Type: Manufacturer.

Product Line: Full line of PCs and notebooks, plus some
                          peripherals, some software. Windows, DOS come
                          preloaded for free. Some bigger systems have free
                          choice of software—check when you order.

Fax: 1-605-232-2023

Information: Catalog (free).

**Orders Accepted
By:**   Phone, mail, fax.

Payment: Cash, check, money order, Visa, MasterCard,
                          American Express, Discover.

Lease Terms:	Yes, Bell Atlantic. Call for details.
Technical Support:	Free lifetime tech support, Monday–Friday: 6 AM–12 midnight; Saturday: 6 AM–5 PM
Delivery:	UPS 2-day ground service or Fed Ex next day (each costs $95).
Guarantees:	Money back within 30 days if not satisfied. 30-day price protection.
On-Site Service:	Free; 1 year.

GLOBAL COMPUTER SUPPLIES

11 Harbor Park Drive
Dept 44
Port Washington, NY 11050

1-800-845-6225
1-516-625-6200 (in NY)

Global may not always be the least expensive solution, but they *do* have everything, from CPUs to computer furniture. If you're looking for a one-stop solution with good prices, Global may be your answer.

Outlet Type:	Catalog house.
Product Line:	Global has some very interesting peripherals, printers and even a few computers, computer furniture and supplies. Global is a complete software supplier, as well, carrying software for Macintosh, DOS, Windows and OS/2 platforms.
Fax:	1-516-625-6683
Information:	Catalog.
Orders Accepted By:	Phone, fax, mail.
Payment:	Check, MasterCard, Visa, American Express. You can also set up a company account and, if approved, be billed.

Delivery:	Fed Ex next day.
Technical Support:	None.
Guarantees:	Satisfaction guaranteed; money refunded if goods returned within 30 days.

GLOBAL HORIZONS, INC.

1051 East High Street
P.O. Box 644
Mundelein, IL 60060

1-800-860-4562
(708) 949-9332 (in IL)

Whoever said that women don't know much about computers never met any of the women who own and operate Global Horizons. This is clearly one of the most knowledgeable teams of people that we've come across. Not only do they sell a broad range of peripherals at really good prices but they are very helpful in the decision-making process. So, if you're one of those people who think that you should support women's businesses this is a great place to shop. And if you're one of those macho know-it-alls who think that only men know about this stuff . . . be prepared for a mind-bending surprise.

Outlet Type:	Catalog house.
Product Line:	Complete peripheral products, plus a small number of laptops.
Fax:	1-708-949-9372
Information:	Catalog.
Orders Accepted By:	Phone, fax, mail.
Payment:	MasterCard, Visa, Discover, wire transfer, check.
Delivery:	UPS. Upgrade to Fed Ex for $3.
Technical Support:	Monday–Friday: 7 AM–6 PM; Saturday: 8 AM–2 PM.
Guarantees:	Money back if returned within 30 days.

IBM PC Direct

3039 Cornwallis Road
Raleigh Technical Park, NC 27709

1-800-IBM-2YOU
1-800-426-2968

Everybody knows the name IBM, but until recently "Big Blue" was charging a significant premium for its name. Not any more: Prices are now competitive with many of the IBM clones. Their technical support is great: Round-the-clock phone service—and if they can't help you over the phone, they'll send a technician to you.

Outlet Type:	Manufacturer.
Product Line:	ThinkPad, ValuePoint, some PC1s and PC2s, printers.
Fax:	1-800-426-4182
Information:	Catalog.
Orders Accepted By:	Phone, mail, fax.
Payment:	Cash, check, Visa, MasterCard, American Express, Discover. No COD.
Lease Terms:	IBM lease: 24- and 36-month.
Technical Support:	24 hours.
Delivery:	UPS 2-day ground service. Airborne overnight delivery at extra charge.
Guarantees:	Money back within 30 days if not satisfied.
On-Site Service:	If they can't help fix the problem over the phone they will send a technician to your office or home.

Inmac

2300 Valley View
Irving, TX 75062

1-800-547-5444
1-800-567-5992 (in Canada)

Inmac has been in business for 18 years and is a big reseller, with highly competitive prices. They also sell their own brand of desktop computers, manufactured for Inmac by IBM's Austin, Texas facility. If Inmac was a store it would easily be considered a "superstore." They have their own tech service via phone, fax or modem.

Outlet Type: Manufacturer.

Product Line: Full line of PCs and notebooks, plus some peripherals. Including but not limited to Toshiba portables, Acer desktops and portables, NEC portables, full AST lines, supplies, software, accessories and peripherals.

Fax: 1-800-972-3210

Information: Catalog (free).

**Orders Accepted
By:**   Phone, mail, fax.

Payment: Cash, check, money order, Visa, MasterCard, American Express.

Lease Terms: Yes. GE Capital Credit. Call for more information.

**Technical
Support:**   Monday–Friday: 6:30 AM–7:30 PM 24-hour a day fax service. BBS electronic bulletin board tech service: Call 1-214-570-4301.

Delivery: Ships custom built systems within 3 days of receipt of your order. They ship via Skyway and have standard charges; ask when ordering.

Guarantees: Money back within 30 days if not satisfied.

On-Site Service: Free for 1 year. Can be extended for three years at anytime during the first year at extra cost.

MICRON COMPUTER, INC./A SUBSIDIARY OF MICRON SEMI-CONDUCTOR

915 East Karcher Road
Nampa, ID 83687

1-800-438-3343
1-208-465-3434 (local)

Micron is fairly new—it was established in 1991—but there are many good reasons to consider it. First, its parent company is a leading memory manufacturer (dram), so memory upgrades are much cheaper. Second: They are one of only two companies allowed by Microsoft to include Microsoft Office 4.2 and MicrosoftWorks in their systems free of charge. [The smaller systems—Model 4333 SVL Valueline (a 486 SX 33) and 4333 VL Magnum (486 DX33) come with MicrosoftWorks included. They can be upgraded to a full version of Microsoft Office for just $100. The bigger systems come with Microsoft Office as part of the system.] Third: All systems come preloaded with the latest version of DOS and Windows, which can save you both money and time.

Outlet Type:	Manufacturer.
Product Line:	Complete line of PCs and notebooks, plus some peripherals. Memory upgrades.
Fax:	1-208-465-3424
Information:	Catalog (free).
Orders Accepted By:	Phone, mail, fax.
Payment:	Check, money order, Visa, MasterCard, American Express, COD; apply over the phone for Micron credit card.
Lease Terms:	Yes, by Leasing Partners. Call for more information.
Technical Support:	Lifetime technical support, Monday–Friday: 7 AM–8 PM; Saturday: 8 AM–5 PM
Delivery:	Fed Ex 2nd day service on preconfigured systems. Custom configured systems will take longer.

Check with sales rep at time of purchase. (On our sample system, Micron quoted us a $69 shipping charge, which they say is fairly standard.)

Guarantees: 30-day money back guarantee.

On-Site Service: 1 year free at Tech Support's discretion within 24 hours, up to 4 years. 3 additional years by GE.

MIDWEST COMPUTER WORKS

180 Lexington Drive
Buffalo Grove, IL 60089

1-800-85-WORKS (1-800-859-6757)

Midwest is a big supplier with a broad product line—it seems there's almost nothing that they don't have. You get the feeling that if there's an item you want but you don't see it listed in the catalog you can just ask for it.

Outlet Type: Catalog house.

Product Line: Complete peripheral products; a number of computers and laptops are also available.

Fax: 1-708-459-6933

Information: Catalog.

Orders Accepted By: Phone, fax, mail.

Payment: MasterCard, Visa, American Express, Discover, checks from approved corporations.

Delivery: Shipped the same day by (your choice): DHL, UPS next day or Fed Ex 2nd day air. Different charges apply.

Technical Support: Yes. 1-708-459-9411.

Guarantees: 30 day return for money back. Limited warranty by Midwest.

NACOMEX

118 East 25th Street
New York, NY 10010

1-212-614-0700 (New York)
1-412-655-9907 (Pittsburgh)
1-210-687-5507 (McAllen, TX)

NACOMEX claims it's the largest computer exchange in the U.S., and it is the only franchised one, with operations in New York, Pittsburgh, Texas—and ones planned for Mexico, Canada and Europe. NACOMEX is a true broker—they never take possession of the computer. Instead, they locate a seller by checking their huge database of available equipment. You then pay a deposit—and pay the balance COD when the computer arrives. NACOMEX handles "every type of computer except no-names," and a large portion of its sales consist of refurbished computers, which come with 90-day manufacturers' warranties and factory tech support.

Outlet Type:	Computer exchange.
Product Line:	New-and-discontinued, refurbished, returned, used and demo models of computers from all major manufacturers, including PCs and Apples.
Fax:	1-212-777-1290.
Information:	Phone.
Orders Accepted By:	Phone, fax.
Payment:	Deposits must be paid by check, wire transfer, or money order. Balance paid COD when computer is delivered.
Delivery:	Seller and buyer arrange delivery.
Technical Support:	Manufacturer's tech support on refurbished equipment. Otherwise, no tech support.
Guarantees:	Manufacturer's warranty on refurbished equipment. All equipment is guaranteed operational, with money back or replacement.

NORTHGATE COMPUTER SYSTEMS

P.O. Box 208
Chaska, MN 55318

1-800-548-1993

In business since 1986, Northgate has won 23 awards from PC publications such as "PC Magazine" and "PC World." They are known worldwide for their high quality tech support. Also, unlike many other suppliers, Northgate still manufactures their own motherboards for their desktop computers—and they always use the newest technology available. This is a very well-made line of computers and is well worth a good look.

Outlet Type:	Manufacturer.
Product Line:	Everything from 486s to Pentiums plus a very good line of notebooks.
Fax:	1-612-361-5181
Information:	Catalog (free).
Orders Accepted By:	Phone, mail, fax.
Payment:	Cash, check, money order, COD with $500 deposit, Visa, MasterCard, American Express, Discover.
Lease Terms:	Yes. Available from 12 months to 4 years. Call for more details.
Technical Support:	Lifetime support, 24-hours a day/seven days a week for life.
Delivery:	Via UPS ground service. Fed Ex next day available at extra charge.
Guarantees:	Money back within 30 days if not satisfied.
On-Site Service:	First year free. 4-year on-site service available for $130 to $260 for up to 4 years.

Ross-Dove Co., Inc.
1241 East Hillsdale Boulevard
Foster City, Ca 94404

1-800-445-DOVE (an electronic listing of all upcoming auctions)

This is one of the most unusual entries in this book. Ross-Dove is an auction house that has a contract with Apple Computer to auction off excess Apple inventory. They hold Macintosh auctions at various cities, at various times. You can get an outstanding bargain if you bid wisely—but note that there won't always be an auction near you, and they can't always guarantee that they will be selling the model you crave. And you won't get a whole heck of a lot of service support. However, if you're in no rush for your Mac and you don't mind traveling a bit for it, they might just have an auction coming up that will interest you. And if you're a PC user, note that Ross-Dove also occasionally gets a shipment of PCs to sell.

To find out what's selling, when and where, call the 800 number above. But be prepared to wait a bit on the phone: When you call you'll get a list of *all* the auctions that are coming up: Jet engines, real estate, spare aircraft parts, etc.

Outlet Type:	Manufacturer.
Product Line:	Macintosh and PCs are auctioned from time to time as well as other computer-related parts and peripherals.
Fax:	1-415-572-1502
Information:	Individual brochures are sent after you phone.
Orders Accepted By:	At auction only. No proxy purchases allowed.
Payment:	25% deposit upon accepted bid. You then have 3 days to pay the balance and remove items. They take cash, cashiers check, wire transfers and charge cards (accepted cards vary from sale to sale).
Lease:	N.A.
Technical Support:	No.
Delivery:	Pick up at auction. You must arrange for your own shipping.

Guarantees:	Guarantees vary from "turn-on warranty" (which just tells you that the thing works) up to full company warranty.
On-Site Service:	No.

USA Flex
471 Brighton Drive
Bloomingdale, IL 60108

1-800-876-5607 or 1-800-333-4515

USA Flex has been in business for 16 years—that's saying something in the competitive world of direct computer sales. There's a reason: They have good quality equipment and competitive pricing, plus a very broad line of peripherals. What's more, they load DOS and Windows into their systems. Check for their occasional specials on software.

Outlet Type:	Manufacturer.
Product Line:	Full line of PCs (486 and up) and notebooks, plus lots peripherals and some software.
Fax:	1-708-351-7204
Information:	Catalog (free).
Orders Accepted By:	Phone, mail, fax.
Payment:	Cash, check, Visa, MasterCard, Discover, American Express, wire transfer, COD.
Lease Terms:	Available. Call for more information.
Technical Support:	24-hours, 7 days a week.
Delivery:	UPS. Fed Ex 2nd-day available at extra charge.
Guarantees:	Money back within 30 days if not satisfied.
On-Site Service:	They charge $70 for the first year. They don't have additional years available at this time, but you can buy additional on-site service separately. Ask for more information.

ZEOS INTERNATIONAL, LTD.

1301 Industrial Boulevard
Minneapolis, MN 55413

1-800-423-5891
1-800-228-5389 (TDD orders)

Zeos is most well-known for delivering products almost in the blink of an eye. Thy claim that 50% of each day's orders are shipped the next day, and most custom configurations are shipped within two to three days. They are also well-known for their quality: For instance, "PC World" has chosen Zeos *Best Buy* three months in a row, and the people at Zeos told us that *PC Magazine* has awarded them their *Readers Choice Award* for service and reliability more times than any other company. Prices are competitive, too.

Outlet Type:	Manufacturer.
Product Line:	Complete line of PCs and notebooks, some peripherals, some software. All machines come with current version of DOS. Machines also come loaded with various software depending on the system program you choose. Each software program is priced differently, but bundling is intended to save you money over third-party purchasing.
Fax:	1-612-633-1325
Information:	Catalog (free).
Orders Accepted By:	Phone, mail, fax.
Payment:	Cash, certified check, money order, Visa, MasterCard, American Express, Discover, wire transfer, or apply for a Zeos credit card.
Lease:	Yes. Bell Atlantic. 36-month lease with 10% buyout option. Call for more information.
Technical Support:	Toll-free 24 hours/7 days a week/365 days a year.

Delivery:	FedEx ($35 notebook, $75 desk, $95 tower); overnight express available for extra charge.
Guarantees:	Money back within 30 days if not satisfied.
On–Site Service:	Yes. $49 for the first year, $99 for each additional year through Dow Jones.

8

Furnishing Your Office

Purchasing office furniture that's sturdy, attractive and, above all, comfortable is important both to your own productivity and your business's growth. For one thing, if you're like most workers, you'll spend three-quarters of your day sitting, so an uncomfortable desk or chair or inadequate lighting can really cramp your style. For another thing, your office furnishings speak volumes to your customers about the state and style of your business. Clearly, furnishing your office is not a decision to be taken lightly, particularly as it can cost you several thousands of dollars, and it's something you must live with, day in and day out.

We know many people, just starting out, who are nervous about spending a lot of money for a well-made desk, a sturdy filing cabinet, a well-designed chair. Instead, they choose cheaper options. We think that's being penny wise and pound foolish. You'll think so too, when that cheap filing cabinet bends and jams, when you get a backache from sitting in an uncomfortable chair, and when that bargain desk shakes every time you lean on it.

The good news is that you can spend less money and still have quality furnishings. This chapter includes discount sources of good quality furniture, but there are other avenues you should explore as well:

- *Check the classified advertising section of newspapers for business liquidation sales.* This is a good source not just of furnishings, but also of computers, phones, small electronics equipment and suppliers.

- *Look for moving sales when large companies change locations, or when they downsize.* When you hear that a company is moving or shrinking, call the office manager, administrative partner, or the office of the Chief Operating Officer to ask if they're selling any unwanted furniture. This can result in amazing bargains. (We know of one person who got a high quality desk, chair, and filing cabinet all for $30!) Tip: A good source of information about moves, downsizes, etc. are commercial real estate brokers. They may be willing to give you this information to build a relationship with you and to provide a service to their clients, who otherwise have to pay to dispose of unwanted furnishings.
- *Shop at garage sales or estate sales.* This can be particularly effective if you want to outfit a home office, as the furnishings are often more "home-like."
- *Don't forget that the U.S. government auctions surplus equipment and supplies!* To learn what's on the block and how you bid, contact the Federal Supply Service, General Services Administration, Washington, D.C. 20406, and the Department of Defense Surplus Sales, P.O. Box 1370, Federal Center, Battle Creek, MI 49016.
- *Sometimes checking the town dump, dumpsters outside office buildings or the collection piles on city streets before "bulk pick up day" can yield treasures!* Desks that just need a coat of paint, carpets that have a piece just right for your office, lighting fixtures, knickknacks, and bookshelves are just some of the things we've seen just for the taking. (Just don't ever admit the source of your furnishings to your clients!)
- *Contact shipping companies to see if they sell slightly damaged furniture, and with storage companies to see if they offer abandoned goods.* Look in the Yellow Pages for shipping and storage companies near you.
- *Check the manufacturers of high-quality office furniture to buy seconds.* They often offer significant discounts; the drawback is that you may have to pay freight, and unless you live close by, you can't inspect before your purchase. Companies to contact:

  - Steelcase
  - Knoll

- *An alternative to dealing directly with manufacturers: Contact local wholesalers of high quality business furniture.* Wholesalers often have a space in their warehouse devoted to "dogs and cats"—that is, ordering mistakes, goods damaged during installation and (sometimes) used furniture. They can't return these goods to the manufacturer, and they're just taking up expensive warehouse space—so make them an offer! In fact, wholesalers can be a good information source, as well, because they know who's upgrading, who's moving and who's downsizing.

- *If you're handy, why not build your own?* You can save money by doing your own assembling and staining. Or if you're really skilled, you could start from scratch, following patterns and suggestions in do-it-yourself books and magazines. (Great if you have odd space you want fit!)
- *Look for mill ends and remnants at flooring and carpet stores.* You can find some real bargains here, especially if you need just a small amount. But don't ever accept their first price—negotiate! We've gotten an additional 20% off and the padding thrown in. A tip: Having cash in hand helps.

As you can see, with a little extra effort and some imaginative searching, you *can* find bargains on office furnishings. But if you're not that adventurous, you can still purchase office furnishings through more traditional channels and save. On the next pages, we provide some sources.

SOURCES:

OFFICE FURNITURE

ADIRONDACK DIRECT

The Adirondack Building
31-01 Vernon Boulevard
Long Island City, NY 11106

1-800-221-2444
1-718-204-4555 (NY call collect)

Adirondack has been in the wholesale furniture business since 1926, and there's a reason: They offer great prices and broad selection. Anything you need for an office—even a portable dance floor!—Adirondack stocks. And they promise to beat any price you've found. They ship all over the U.S. and throughout the world. Whether you're looking for basics or executive suite furnishings, Adirondack will have it, and they'll back it up with a 15-year guarantee on many products. If you pay by check, you can take off an additional 4%—something that can really add up if you're furnishing an entire office. Finally, for those who really want to save, they offer used furniture at their retail outlets at a substantial discount.

Outlet Type:	Catalog house, retail outlets.
Product Line:	Full line of office furniture and furnishings, including executive chairs (leather and fabric), desks, credenzas, conference tables, bookcases, office panels, reception area seating, conference seating, administrative assistant seating, stacking chairs, file systems, utility stands, audio visual tables, display racks, display cases, steel shelving, platforms and risers, coat racks, protective mats, folding and roll-away tables, table skirting, portable dance floors, food service seating, design your own tables, lecterns, signage boards, computer workstations, more.

Fax:	1-800-477-1330
Information:	Catalog (free).
Orders Accepted By:	Phone, fax, mail, in-store.
Payment:	Check in advance (additional 4% discount), Adirondack account, Visa, MasterCard, American Express.
Delivery:	Shipping charges are FOB nearest shipping point (tailgate); for inside delivery there is an additional charge of $9.75. Usually UPS.
Guarantees:	Up to 15-year guarantee, depending on product. Also, if you see the same product somewhere else for a lower price they will beat price.

BUSINESS & INSTITUTIONAL FURNITURE COMPANY, INC.

611 North Broadway
Milwaukee, WI 53202-0902

1-800-558-8662
1-800-242-7200 (in Wisconsin)

B&I offers a broad line of office furniture at extremely competitive prices. In fact, they guarantee they will meet or beat competitors' prices on products that are the same as those in its catalog. What's more, if you're confused about how to set up your office, B&I offers space planning and design *absolutely free*. This service is performed by its in-house design department, and is available for any size project—from a one-room office to a major expansion/relocation. What's more, if you need more information before you buy, B&I is happy to send you free product literature, color samples and fabric swatches. And everything's backed up by a hefty 15-year guarantee.

Outlet Type:	Catalog house.
Product Line:	Executive chairs (leather and fabric), desks, credenzas, conference tables, bookcases, office panels, reception area seating, conference seating, administrative assistant seating, stacking chairs, file systems, utility stands, display racks, display cases,

steel shelving, coat racks, protective mats, folding and roll-away tables, table skirting, signage boards, computer workstations, more.

Fax: 1-800-468-1526

Information: Catalog (free).

Orders Accepted By: Phone, fax, mail (P.O. Box 92069, Milwaukee, WI 53202-0069).

Payment: Check, money order in advance (deduct 1% extra discount), company account (30-day billing), MasterCard, Visa, Discover. Offers volume discounts.

Delivery: Shipping is extra. FOB shipping point. Inside delivery is extra. They will provide an estimate of these charges before order is shipped.

Guarantees: 15-year guarantee. They will match or beat other vendors.

FACTORY DIRECT FURNITURE

225 East Michigan Street
Milwaukee, WI 53202

1-800-972-6570
1-414-289-9770 (in Milwaukee)

Factory Direct offers a good selection of core office furniture, all at savings of 20–70% off manufacturers' suggested retail prices. What's more, they'll meet or beat competitors' prices on furniture carried in their catalog. They have a good selection of brand-name office furniture, including Chairworld, Thomasville, La-Z-Boy and more. You can really furnish your office on a budget here, and it helps that they provide free office planning and free color samples before you buy. Note that Factory Direct offers only a 5–7-year guarantee on some products (but others have a lifetime guarantee).

Outlet Type: Catalog house.

Product Line: Executive chairs (leather and fabric), desks, credenzas, conference tables, bookcases, office panels, reception area seating, conference seating, administrative assistant seating, stacking chairs, file systems, utility stands, display racks, display cases, steel shelving, coat racks, protective mats, folding and roll away tables, signage boards, computer workstations and more.

Fax:
1-414-289-9946.

Information:
Catalog (free).

**Accepts Orders
By:**
Phone, fax, mail.

Payment:
Check, money order (50% deposit required), offers company charge account, American Express, Visa, MasterCard.

Delivery:
Some items are shipped by UPS, some bigger items are shipped by truck. Inside delivery is extra. Delivery is 3–4 weeks, but 1–2 weeks on some marked items.

Guarantees:
Depends on products; ranges from 5 years to lifetime. Will meet or beat competitor's price on identical products. Proof of competitor's current price must accompany with order.

FRANK EASTERN CO.

599 Broadway
New York, NY 10012-3258

1-800-221-4914
1-212-219-0007 (in NY)

This is one of our favorite places to shop—maybe because we've been in the showroom and have purchased from them. They may not have the biggest selection, but what they have is first class stuff. And they offer very good prices, 25–60% off retail.

Outlet Type:
Catalog house.

Product Line:
Executive chairs (leather and fabric), desks, credenzas, conference tables, bookcases, office panels, reception area seating, conference seating,

administrative assistant seating, stacking chairs, file systems, utility stands, display racks, display cases, wood or steel shelving, coat racks, protective mats, folding and roll-away tables, signage boards, computer workstations.

Fax: 1-212-219-0722

Information: Catalog (free).

Orders Accepted By: Phone, fax, mail, in-store.

Payment: Charge account, check or money order, Visa, MasterCard.

Delivery: Some items are marked free delivery. UPS is used wherever possible. Trucking deliveries on bulkier items carry an additional inside delivery charge. Advance telephone notice of delivery is $5.

Guarantees: Many items have extended guarantees—ask when buying. Frank Eastern provides a money-back guarantee against defects and damages.

GLOBAL BUSINESS FURNITURE

22 Harbor Park Drive
Dept 9410
Port Washington, NY 11050

1-800-472-0101

Global offers a full line of office furniture. Prices are competitive. They will also develop custom-built or customized furniture for your office, so you can get the high-quality furniture and look you want specifically for your space.

Outlet Type: Catalog house.

Product Line: Executive chairs (leather and fabric), desks, credenzas, bookcases, office panels, reception area seating, conference seating, administrative assistant seating, stacking chairs, file systems, utility stands, audio visual tables, display racks, display cases, steel shelving, platforms and risers, coat racks, protective mats, folding and roll-away tables, food service seating, signage boards, computer workstations.

Fax: 1-800-336-3818

Information: Catalog (free).

**Orders Accepted
By:**   Phone, fax, mail.

Payment: Check in advance, company account (must be approved) MasterCard, Visa, American Express.

Delivery: Freight FOB shipping point. Shipping via UPS or common carrier.

Guarantees: 30-day money back guarantee (including freight if shipped via UPS). Custom-built or cut items are excluded.

LANGLEY CO.

2 Sycamore Avenue
Medford, MA 02155

1-800-225-4499
1-617-395-8010 (in New England)

This is not your normal furniture outlet. Langley focuses on industrial environments. Although they don't have a very big selection of regular office furniture, they more than make up for it in the number of interesting things they *do* carry for industrial (plant) workspaces. They also offer material and handling equipment, and safety and maintenance equipment. The prices are competitive and Langley offer a lot of furnishings that other vendors don't offer.

Outlet Type: Catalog house.

Product Line: Moderate selection of office furniture, broad selection of plant and industrial shelving, storage, materials handling and safety and maintenance equipment.

Fax: 1-800-343-4291

Information: Catalog (free).

**Orders Accepted
By:**   Phone, fax, mail.

Payment: Checks, open accounts (for approved customers),
                       American Express, MasterCard, Visa.

Delivery: Shipments are made prepaid freight. A $9.50
                       handling charge applies to all prepaid freight and
                       COD orders.

Guarantees: 30-day, no-questions-asked money-back guarantee
                       on stock items (freight charges included).

Also see Chapters 11 and 12.

9

Information

Information is the lifeblood of business. We use it to set long-term strategies, find and understand our customers and suppliers, develop marketing plans, penetrate new markets, set pricing and so much more. Information helps us hone our decisions and reduce the risks of doing business.

If information is our lifeblood, it's safe to say that the blood supply is increasing. We live in the Information Age, a place where a couple of keystrokes gets us access to vast realms of knowledge, where computers around the globe are linked to each other through the world of Cyberspace, where supercomputers gather trillions of bytes of data on every subject imaginable. Today, the amount and variety of information available to businesses is absolutely staggering. *But the great news is that much of this information is free or at very low cost.*

This chapter focuses on how to access low cost or free information sources, as well as how to minimize the costs of using on-line services and the Internet.

Finding Free or Low-Cost Information from the Federal Government

Looking for information on how to do business in Togo? How to patent a product? Who's producing dairy products? Ways to increase your company's productivity? Population growth estimates for the mature market or the Hispanic community? Or the size of the U.S. market for shoes, computers or any of more than 2000 other products? The federal government can help, with free or extremely low cost information.

But how can you find it in the labyrinth of Washington? In which of the thousands of agencies, departments, offices and centers do you focus your search? Below, we provide some tips:

1. *Start your search with the mother lode: The Commerce Department.* The Department of Commerce's charter is to "encourage, serve and promote economic development and technological advancement" and to "provide social and economic statistics and analyses for business"—so it's the logical first step. Virtually every department will be chock full of experts and statistics germane to small businesses, but we particularly recommend:

   International Trade Administration (information on how to export, overseas market sizes, country regulations, help for exporters, market size and growth prospects for 15 industries in 20 countries): 1-202-482-2000.

   Bureau of Economic Analysis (tracks market size and trends): 1-202-606-9900.

   Office of Economic Affairs (tracks overall economic trends and their likely impact on various industries): 1-202-377-3523.

   Bureau of the Census (population growth rates, trends characteristics, income, etc.): 1-301-763-7662.

   National Technical Information Service (sponsors research into, and sells research reports about, advanced technology): 1-703-306-1040.

   Minority Business Development Agency (assists minority businesses in succeeding in business): 1-202-482-5741.

   Patent and Trademark Office (sells copies of issued documents that can provide significant information about product capabilities and design): 1-703-557-3158.

   • If you have a quick question about commerce and business, the U.S. Department of Commerce Library provides a free reference service. They'll check standard business reference books to get you information on companies, and provide telephone numbers for overseas businesses. Call the library at 1-202-482-2000, or write Library, Department of Commerce, Washington, D.C. 20230.

- For more information on the multitude of services, reports, statistics, computerized databases, and expert information available from the Department of Commerce, we suggest that you obtain the free publication, *"Business Services Directory."* This publication lists all the agencies and departments, tells what they do, and provides contacts and telephone numbers. Get it through the Office of Business Liaison, Department of Commerce, Rm 5062, Washington, D.C. 20230; telephone 1-202-482-1360.

2. ***Obtain one-stop data sources from the government.*** Two publications can help you avoid making expensive and time-consuming phone calls in order to find out basic information: *"The Statistical Abstract of the United States"* and *"U.S. Industrial Outlook."* The Abstract compiles key information on population, industry, education, housing, health, the economy, etc. from all the major U.S. government agencies. The Outlook provides a look ahead at 300+ U.S. industries, as well as providing names, telephone numbers, and addresses of industry experts. Obtain these from Superintendent of Documents, U.S. Government Printing Office, Washington, D.C. 20402; telephone 1-202-783-3238.

3. ***Finally, focus on your particular topic of inquiry.*** After you've gotten your feet wet with the various Department of Commerce offerings, we suggest that you begin to focus your search by contacting the agencies that concentrate on the industry in which you're interested. In the "Sources" section, we've listed the various topics in which a small business might be interested, the departments and agencies that handle these subjects and their telephone numbers.

The listings in the "Sources" section will give you a taste of what's available when the U.S. government puts your corporate tax dollars to work. If you want more detailed information on what Uncle Sam has to offer, we suggest you look at *Information U.S.A.,* by Matthew Lesko (Penguin Books, NY). It's a wonderful 1200-page guide to government information and programs, and well worth its $24.95 price tag.

Using Other Data Sources

There are numerous other rich sources of data, including:

1. ***Industry Associations.*** You'd be amazed at the type and number of industry associations. There are ice cream manufacturers, fireplace

makers, even an association of "Groovers and Grinders" (involving road resurfacing, not striptease!). Many associations compile statistics and commission market study—and may make this information available to the general public at little or no charge. (Sometimes you have to join the association—but that's often a cost-effective way to obtain information that would cost you hundreds or thousands of dollars on the open market.)

The best way to find out if there's an industry group is to check Gale's *Directory of Associations* at your local library. Once you get in touch with the industry association, ask for the library or information service. If they don't have one, ask for the press relations or director's office.

2. *State and Local Governments.* Particularly if it's an industry of importance to the area (such as dairy farming in Wisconsin or gaming in Nevada), state or local bodies often gather statistics and perform market studies. The best place to start is with your state's Office of Economic Development. We provide a list of these offices in Chapter 3, "Business Consulting Services."

3. *Industry Experts.* Why reinvent the wheel? Usually, there are people who already know practically everything there is to know about a subject. And because it's their passion, they're happy to share their knowledge with someone else who shows an interest. (For instance, we've been amazed and gratified at the experts who have happily given us all sorts of information as we have gathered material for this book!) The key is to find these experts. Some tips:

   - Talk to people at the trade associations. They often have a list of experts to whom they refer the press and other interested parties.
   - Editors and writers at trade journals are usually well-versed in a field and can serve as experts. They also have lists of expert contacts.
   - Call the people quoted in the press or who have written books on the subject.
   - Check sources and bibliographies of books on the subject. They often cite interviews. And note: They also often cite market studies and other data.

4. *Librarians.* In general, good librarians are worth their weight in gold. They'll point you to great reference books, help you do a literature search, and walk you through the maze of on-line databases and other computerized information that good libraries now have. But when

you find a librarian who specializes in your particular area, you have found an absolutely solid-platinum resource. You'll find these librarians in association libraries, at universities and (sometimes) in business sections of public libraries.

5. ***Publications.*** Books, magazines, and newspapers can be great sources. The trick is to learn to use the card catalogs and abstract directories, such as the "Readers' Guide to Periodic Literature," to find writings of interest to you. Your librarian can help.

Saving Money on On-Line Services

These days, you need never leave your desk to use one of the fastest and most convenient ways to get information: on-line services. But these services can be quite expensive—so it's key to find ways to keep costs down. Some tips:

1. ***Pick your on-line service carefully.*** You want to choose an on-line service that has the information you want and gives you easy, quick access to key databases. You also need a service that doesn't charge an arm and a leg, and one that provides good, easy-to-use, low-cost e-mail. Finally, you want a service that can support a high access speed; this will greatly reduce your time-use and telephone line charges. In the "Sources" section, we provide our assessment of five on-line service suppliers at this writing.

2. ***Reduce on-line charges.*** A number of hints:

   • *Get the fastest modem you can.* Modems work at different baud speeds—the higher the speed, the faster they can transmit or receive data. So a faster modem can save you money on both phone line time and on-line time. The extra $100 you spend now on a higher-speed modem will be recouped in a very short time because your download time will be decreased. (For example: A file that takes one hour to download at 2400 baud will only take about 15 minutes at 14,400 baud).

   • *If you're gaining access to an on-line service via a local call, call from a residential line.* Depending on the area, some phone companies charge residential lines a flat fee, but business calls a per-minute fee. For example, A residential call from a NYC number to another NYC number is only 11¢ during the day for as long as you want. A business call is 9¢ a minute. Can you make that on-line call from home?

- *If the local number you call to access the service only supports a lower baud rate, consider finding a nearby city that can support a higher baud rate.* If you're paying a high per-minute on-line charge, this can work to save you money. Even though the access call is long distance, it can still be cheaper in the long run because the time on-line will be decreased.
- *Make sure you don't leave it connected.* We know someone who went home as something was downloading, then went on a business trip. Needless to say, the impact on the bottom line was disastrous.
- *Know what you're looking for.* It's fun to browse—but it can be extremely expensive. Before you get on-line, develop a list of keywords and try these first. Try not to get distracted: Keep the search focused.

3. ***Join a BBS.*** BBS are electronic bulletin board services that are growing in scope and importance, and they're surprisingly low-cost to join. (Some are even free!) Bulletin boards are often focused on a single interest, such as business or commodities, any one of several thousand different areas. They allow you to talk to others who have the same interests as you, gain information, ask questions, and even access stock quotations, business/company information and more. It takes a little digging, that's all. To find out what's available, check two magazines: *Boardwatch* and *"Computer Shopper"* (see the on-line section in the latter). *"On-Line Access"* often has listings of new bulletin boards.

4. ***Use the Internet.*** We don't have space to get into a discussion of Cyberspace here, but suffice it to say that we think it's going to be one of the greatest sources of information for business in the next five years. The Internet is a loosely connected network of unrelated computers and their databases. Although anyone who has a registered Internet address can access or be accessed in the Internet, It has been used, historically, as an important link between universities, research institutions, government agencies, etc. But businesses have glommed onto this system recently, and business use is growing. Some caveats:

- The Internet is not for the faint of heart. It can be very difficult and time-consuming to learn. If you can't find what you want on the service of your choice, but you only need to look in the

Internet once in a while, Call Delphi and ask for a Internet search company in your area.

- Most small businesses rarely, if ever, truly *need* the full access to the Internet, although many people say it's addictive to "surf" it. Most business-related data can be found on any of the commercial services. There's some very heady stuff available on CompuServe, GEnie and Dow Jones.

- If you really feel compelled to go surfing on the Internet, there are a number of books you should read and magazines you should look into:

  - *Boardwatch*

  - *On-Line Access*

SOURCES:

INFORMATION

U.S. Government Sources

Topic	Agency / Department	How to Contact	Other Information
Market Size, Dynamics, Growth Rates, Consumer Trends, Etc.	• Int'l Trade Commission	• 1-202-205-2000	• Produces about 100 market studies per year; particularly good on volume of domestic vs. imported goods. Free.
	• Gen'l Accounting Office	• 1-202-512-3000	• Conducts special audits and inquiries at the request of the U.S. Congress on a variety of

Topic	Agency/Department	How to Contact	Other Information
			topics; produces well over 500 per year, on everything from why new home costs are so high to how to encourage deep ocean mining. Free for first copy of reports/$1 after.
	• Central Intelligence Agency	• 1–703–482–1100	• Provides declassified reports on a variety of topics, including energy statistics, information on foreign countries' technology and purchasing patterns, and more. Prices vary.
	• Congressional Committee Hearings	• Call the House Bill Status Office to see if a hearing on your topic has ever been held, 1–202–224–3121. Or check the *Congressional*	• Congress holds thousands of hearings each year on all types of topics: baby boomers, health care, energy, shipping, and much

Topic	Agency/Department	How to Contact	Other Information
		Information Service Index at most libraries.	more. Copies of transcripts can be obtained free directly from the Congressional committee, or with a small charge from the Superintendent of Documents, Government Printing Office, 1-202-783-3238.
	• Congressional Research Service	• Obtain reports through your congressional representative's office.	• Develops over 1000 reports a year to support legislators with information they need on a variety of topics. Reports are free.
	• Federal Trade Commission	• 1-202-326-2222.	• Develops reports on industries the FTC is studying for possible antitrust violations. Fee: 10¢ per page.
	• Bureau of Labor Statistics, Department of Labor	• 1-202-606-5886	• Provides information on employment, prices,

Topic	Agency / Department	How to Contact	Other Information
			living conditions, productivity and OSHA.
	• National Center for Education Statistics	• 1-202-254-6057	• Provides information on levels of schooling, subjects taken, computers and other technology in the schools, etc.
	• Estimates Division and Economics and Statistics, Department of Agriculture	• 1-202-720-2791	• Provides agricultural production and food consumption statistics and projections.
Competition Check out sources that cover specific industries or activities:	• Department of Transportation	• 1-202-366-4000	• Airlines
	• Federal Reserve System	• 1-202-452-3000	• Banking
	• Office of Thrift Supervision	• 1-202-906-6000	• Banking
	• Consumer Product Safety Comm.	• 1-301-492-6608	• Consumer Products

Topic	Agency/Department	How to Contact	Other Information
	• Department of Commerce, World Traders Reports Section	• 1-202-482-2000	• Exporting Companies; Foreign Corporations
	• Food and Drug Administration	• 1-301-443-1594	• Food, Pharmaceuticals and Cosmetics
	• SEC	• 1-202-942-8090	• Public Companies
	• Congressional Caucus for Science and Technology	• 1-202-226-7788	• Provides Congress with information about technology use, growth trends, and impact on U.S. businesses; publishes summaries and newsletters.
Technology	• International Trade Administration, Department of Commerce	• 1-202-482-2000	• Has developed profiles on U.S. high technology industries such as biotechnology, computers, telecommunications, semiconductors and more. Free.

Topic	Agency / Department	How to Contact	Other Information
	• National Technical Information Service	• 1-703-487-4600	• The mother lode for technological advice, but this service charges for its releases. (Sometimes, you can get the same report from the U.S. Government Printing Office for far less!) However, the NTIS is the central source for all U.S.-sponsored research and general technological information. The collection exceeds 1,000,000 titles, and 60,000 more are added annually.
	• Research Resources Information Center, Department of Health and Human Services	• 1-301-594-7938	• Free directory summarizes the biotechnology research that's being carried out

Topic	Agency/Department	How to Contact	Other Information
			throughout the U.S., with contact names.
	• National Institute of Health	• 1-301-496-5787	• Each of the 12 different institutes that comprise the NIH focuses on different aspects of medicine; experts within these institutes can assist you in tracking down information on biotechnology relevant to their field of expertise.
	• Office of Productivity and Technology Studies, Dept. of Labor	• 1-202-606-5603	• Issues reports on the impact of technological changes on employment, productivity, ways of competing, etc.
	• National Referral Center, Library of Congress	• 1-202-707-5000	• Maintains an on-line referral service of 12,000+ experts who are willing to provide information to the

Topic	Agency / Department	How to Contact	Other Information
			general public on technology and science.
Import/Export	• Bureau of the Census	• 1–202–763–7662	• Provides detailed statistical analyses of overseas markets, as well as demographics, import/export figures and marketing research consultation.
	• Import/Export Bank of the U.S.	• 1–202–622–9823	• Maintains credit information on thousands of foreign firms.
	• Office of International Economic Policy, International Trade Administration	• 1–202–482–3022	• Experts can provide marketing and regulatory information on the countries they track.
	• Office of U.S. and Foreign Commercial Service, International Trade Administration	• 1–202–482–5777	• Provides information on government programs aimed at encouraging exporting and provide assistance in all phases of

Topic	Agency/Department	How to Contact	Other Information
			the export process. There are 47 local offices in the U.S. and 124 posts abroad; call for location nearest you.
	• International Population Division, Center for International Research, Bureau of Census	• 1–301–763–7662	• Provides information on population, trends and demographics of various countries.
	• Office of International Trade, Small Business Administration	• 1–202–205–7701	• Provides information on assistance available to small businesses as they attempt to export, and has a number of low-cost pamphlets that provide step-by-step guides. Of note: *"Market Overseas with U.S. Government Help,"* a free publication that describes the various agencies that offer assistance.

Topic	Agency/Department	How to Contact	Other Information
	• International Trade Administration	• 1-202-482-3809	• Provides a variety of information. Ask for *"Foreign Market Reports,"* which offer information on markets for specific products in foreign countries.
	• Market Research Division, Department of Commerce	• 1-202-482-2000	• Ask them for *"Global Market Surveys,"* which analyze overseas markets for their potential and identifies the best ones.

On-Line Services

Supplier	Information	Ease of Use	Cost	Access	e-mail	Overall
America On-Line, 8619 Westwood Center Drive, Vienna, VA 22182-2285 1-800-827-6364	Fewer business-focused databases than other suppliers.	Extremely easy to use.	Moderate monthly fee includes 5 hrs. of free on-line time.	9600 baud maximum.	Excellent, easy to use, and free.	If you have intense information needs, this is not for you.

Supplier	Information	Ease of Use	Cost	Access	e-mail	Overall
CompuServe P.O. Box 20212, Columbus, OH 43220; 1–800–848-8199	Wonderful range of business databases.	Almost too much information; can be difficult to find what you want. Some new software has reduced some confusion.	Low monthly cost and unlimited access to news, stock quotes, general reference, but high fees to use Forums.	14,400 baud maximum.	Excellent, but there is a moderate charge.	Wonderful information source for business, but can be pricey, and can be almost too much to handle.
Dow Jones News/Retrieval with MCI Mail Dow Jones: P.O. Box 300, Princeton, NJ 08543–0300; 1–609-452-1511. MCI Mail: #700, 1133 19th St., N.W., Washington, DC 20036; 1–800–444-6245.	Wonderful range of business databases; particularly strong on financials and corporate reports, as well as the Text Library, that gives you full-text access to more than 1600 publications.	Software has made accessing this huge database somewhat easier, but it still takes some knowledge.	Highest cost: big monthly fee ($29.95/month) and high timed fees (can be over $60/hour!).	9600 baud maximum.	Excellent, but it's a separate account, and charges are highest of any service.	OK for big business and or if your business runs on information (e.g., consulting, investing), but small business people don't need this expense.

Supplier	Information	Ease of Use	Cost	Access	e-mail	Overall
GEnie, 401 N. Washington St. P. O. Box 6403 Rockville, MD 20849, 1-800-638-9636	Access to Dialog, TRW corporate credit files, and a gateway to Dow Jones News Retrieval means this is great for the high-information-need business.	Menu-driven. But some users have issues with the access to forums.	Moderate monthly fees; the real problem is the high usage cost to access the databases.	9600 baud maximum	More difficult to use than other services, but does allow you to download messages to your computer for storage. And there's no charge for e-mail.	Convenient for information-intensive businesses, but the databases are no real bargain.
Prodigy, 445 Hamilton Avenue, White Plains, NY 10601, 1-800-Prodigy.	Good basic information, but not as much detail as some businesses need. Includes Dow Jones, business and finance news—but not access to serious databases.	Interface is "OK but a little crowded"; can be difficult to figure out what's available. Also, sometimes can be slow.	Fees are higher than the other consumer-focused service, America On-Line, but they *do* give you unlimited access to core services and two hours of Plus features.	9600 baud maximum.	More difficult to use than other providers, and currently allows only 30 free messages per month—after that, it's a whopping 25¢ per message.	Good for basic information needs and low-level e-mail use, but others are better if your needs in either area are more intense.

10

Marketing, Promotion and Advertising

"You have to spend money to make money." Many people use that old saying to justify spending significant amounts on marketing-related activities. Are they correct?

Well, yes and no. Certainly, it pays to invest in *effective* marketing—that is, marketing that creates short-term revenues and/or builds the long-term competitive strength of your company. Cutting corners on some things—like strength of your design or the quality of your printed materials—can be penny wise and pound foolish. You don't have to go overboard, but if your advertising layout screams "cheap!" when your intended message is "quality goods," you'll confuse the customer and possibly make him or her a little less likely to buy.

So, this chapter isn't about how to cut marketing corners. Rather, it's about how to cut marketing *fat*. Simply put, you don't have to pay top dollar on things like advertising, promotion, trade shows and public relations to get great results.

Before we move on to our discussion, we need to point out that marketing is a huge subject, and we only have space to talk about the very tip of the iceberg here. So we suggest that you do some more digging. For instance, if you'd like more information about *general marketing,* we recommend the following books, because they're specifically tailored to small businesses' needs and marketing budgets:

- *Guerilla Marketing* and *Guerilla Marketing Weapons* by Jay Conrad Levinson, Plume Books, New York, NY.
- *The Frugal Marketer* by J. Donald Weinrauch and Nancy Croft Baker, AMACOM Press. You can order this at 1-800-538-4761.

If you'd like some information on specific aspects of advertising or marketing, a suggestion: Make your first stop the professional association associated with these disciplines. They usually have free or low-cost information for businesses, a recommended bibliography and helpful people at the other end of the line.

Addresses for key marketing-related associations:

- *American Marketing Association,* 250 South Wacker Drive, Suite 200, Chicago, IL 60606. Telephone: 1-312-648-0536.
- *Association of National Advertisers,* 155 East 44th Street, New York, NY 10017. Telephone: 1-212-697-5950.
- *Direct Marketing Association,* 11 West 42nd Street, New York, NY 10036-8096. Telephone: 1-212-768-7277.
- *International Exhibitors Association,* 5501 Backlick Road, Suite 105, Springfield, VA 22151. Telephone: 1-703-941-3725.
- *Public Relations Society of America,* 33 Irving Place, 3rd Floor, New York, NY 10003-2376. Telephone: 1-212-995-2230.
- *Trade Show Bureau,* 1660 Lincoln Street, Suite 2080, Denver, CO 80264. Note: Offers a variety of "how-to" reports at low cost ($5 and up). Telephone: 1-303-860-7626; fax 1-303-860-7479.
- *Yellow Pages Publishers Association,* 820 Kirts Blvd., Ste. 100, Troy, MI 48084. Telephone: 1-810-244-6200.

Below, we discuss some specific ways you can save on your marketing expenditures.

General Marketing Advice

The most effective and efficient marketing efforts include good planning, clear goal-setting and ways to track marketing performance. It also helps if you can develop some good marketing alliances—and if you aim your marketing efforts at targets that will really pay off. Below, we provide some tips to help build overall marketing performance.

1. ***Develop a marketing plan before you do anything.*** The road to good marketing is fraught with pitfalls, and even big marketers break an axle or two in them. What can go wrong? Sometimes, businesses don't spend enough to create awareness—and wonder why no one responds to their ads. Other times, they may follow a "boom and bust" spending strategy that doesn't provide a consistent presence. They may choose media that don't reach the target audience. Their message may be ho-hum—not particularly exciting to the target market, or too similar to what the competition is offering. Or they put all their eggs in one basket—say, newspaper advertising—without even considering the other ways they might get the word out.

   The hard truth is that nothing can *totally* prevent you from making those mistakes. Marketing is as much art as science—and even as a science, there's still a lot of trial-and-error experimenting going on.

   But there *is* one way to help minimize mistakes and maximize effectiveness, and that's to develop a marketing plan. Developing a marketing plan will provide you with guidelines and a clear direction for your efforts, and it'll stop you from going down a lot of blind alleys. When done right, it can ensure that all the different marketing activities work together to create synergy. It entails five steps:

   1) Figure out what you want to be in the marketplace—who you're targeting, what your benefits are, why you're better than the competition.

   2) Determine your marketing *strategy:* that is, how you're going to use promotion and advertising, product line, pricing, your distribution levers and your image in the marketplace to gain a competitive advantage that results in more customers.

   3) Write a marketing plan that outlines what you're going to do and how you're going to do it. Include a detailed budget in this plan and specific goals for all marketing efforts.

   4) Execute the plan.

   5) Monitor how well you've done and make changes in your on-going marketing efforts in response to this feedback.

   Putting the time and thought into developing a marketing plan may not be as easy as just going along—but it's the cornerstone of efficient and effective marketing. Believe us, it will save you more money and result in more sales than any of the other tips we provide below.

2. ***Make sure you can track marketing effectiveness.*** John Wanamaker, founder of the great department store chain, once said, "Half of my advertising works. I only wish I knew which half." Don't get into this situation. Before you launch an advertising campaign, display at a trade show or embark on a public relations campaign, sit down and figure out how you will measure how well it's working. That way, you can direct your marketing budget to the activities that have the best payoff for your business. *This is one of the keys to efficient marketing!*

What should you measure, and how should you do it? Let's take those questions one at a time.

What you measure really depends on your goals for that particular marketing activity. Of course, marketing's ultimate goal is to *create customers,* but there's a lot that has to happen to do so: making people aware of your existence; separating yourself out from other competitors; creating an image and letting people know the benefits of doing business with you; encouraging trial; developing repeat business; and creating awareness of and attendance at specific events, such as sales.

How you measure it can vary. If you're measuring awareness of your brand name, you may need to do a consumer survey to see who in your target audience knows your name and understands what you offer. If you want to find out if an ad pulled people into your store during a sale event, you could simply compare sales pre-event, during the event, and post-event. A better method, however, is to ask customers and browsers alike what brought them into the store. (Why is this better? Because sometimes an ad pulls beautifully—but when people get there, they don't like the merchandise, can't find their size, or are disappointed with the discount or the service. The ad did its work, but other things were awry.) If you want to see whether a trade show creates new business, you might track new leads, new conversions or total sales from new conversions.

One thing that's particularly helpful in tracking effectiveness is to *include a response mechanism* in your marketing efforts. We're talking about things like, "Bring this ad in for an extra discount" (or free gift, or chance to win a dinner for two). Remember, if you're running that ad in several publications, you'll have to put different codes on each of the different ads in order to tell its source. If you have a telemarketing operation, your operators can ask where the caller got the information, or what catalog they're ordering from. Then, you can collect this information and track the relative efficiency and return on your marketing investment.

Understanding what advertising media and what messages are working is absolutely critical, because it tells you where to direct your marketing dollars and what to say. All the large direct marketers do it, because it makes good business sense. Take a lesson from them.

3. ***Get good marketing partners—your advertising and public relations agencies.*** It's critical to locate agencies that will help you think through marketing issues, bring new ideas and techniques to the table, work with you on creating a professional, exciting and consistent image and ensure that you communicate compelling offers to your target market. You need agencies that are both smart and service-oriented—and, of importance, aren't merely focused on creating an image for you—they'll do the nitty-gritty marketing that results in more *sales.*

4. ***Start with marketing to your current customers.*** Repeat customers drive the profitability of every business in the world except one: funeral homes. That's why airlines invented frequent flyer clubs, and why everyone from bookstores to hotels to department stores are following in their footsteps. They know it's far easier to sell to a customer they already have than to convince someone to become a customer, and that loyal customers are worth their weight in gold. If you haven't figured this out yet, you're in for a treat: Merely by marketing directly to your current customer base, you can significantly increase the profitability of your business.

If you haven't captured customer information yet, start now. You'll want to capture not only name and address, but other things, such as product preferences. We urge you to computerize this using a simple database program, because a database will give you an easy way to sort and select the specific customers you want to talk to.

Once you have customer information, you can develop targeted mailings and service offerings. You can create your own frequent purchase club, or "preferred customer" group. You can enhance your relationship by sending birthday cards (if you've captured birthdate!), thank you notes, notices of special sales and advance notice of new merchandise.

All this will translate into a cost-effective way to increase sales the easy way: by marketing to your current customers.

5. ***Look for comarketers.*** A cosponsor can really help you stretch your dollars and dramatically improve your marketing impact. The trick is to find ones that are targeting a similar audience and can offer your customers noncompeting benefits. If you own a children's clothing

store, for instance, you might team up with a book store and a toy store to form a "children's club" where members get special offers and discounts in all three places, as well as personalized items on their birthday. If you provide computer consulting, you might put together a discount deal with the local software retailer. Restaurateurs might team up with the wine store, typing agencies with the copy shop, personal trainers with the athletic shoe store.

Forming this kind of alliance affords many benefits. For one thing, it enhances your offer. What's more, if you pool advertising funds, it makes you look more substantial. It gives you access to your partners' mailing lists—chock full of names and addresses of your target audience. And it gives you access to good ideas your partners may have come up with—many that are worth their weight in gold.

Advertising Tips

From finding co-op dollars to creatively cutting production costs to experimenting with new, inexpensive media, there are many methods for reducing advertising expense. Here are some interesting ones.

1. *Check out co-op advertising opportunities.* Co-op ads can be a wonderful way to stretch your advertising dollars. Every year, manufacturers set aside millions and millions of dollars in cooperative advertising funds to be used by their distribution channels—wholesalers, distributors and retailers. Typically, the way it works is that you earn an advertising credit of 3–5% on your purchases from the supplier. This credit accrues and can be used to partially offset the costs of advertising.

   There are some caveats—the money sort of grows on trees, but you have to cultivate it a little. You usually will have to follow some advertising guidelines to qualify—like featuring the manufacturer prominently, having an ad that conforms to a certain "look," or not mentioning competitors. Generally, you have to front the money for the space or time; the manufacturer will reimburse you when you show tear sheets or confirmation of broadcast. And getting the money entails completing paperwork, although how much or how little depends on manufacturers' various policies.

   Co-op advertising dollars can be used in all sorts of media—print, broadcast, outdoor and Yellow Pages. It's particularly easy to glom onto Yellow Page co-op dollars, because the "Yellow Pages Co-op Advertising Programs" directory provides a one-stop source for details on hundreds of co-op programs. The Yellow Pages Publishers Association in Troy, Michigan publishes it and updates it several times a year. Contact the YPPA at 1-313-680-8880 or ask your Yellow Pages rep for a copy of the directory to look at. (Note: You may have to push to see this. Yellow Pages ad reps make less commission on these ads, so some are not wildly forthcoming with this information).

2. ***Try arranging for trade-outs.*** If you sell something useful to broadcasters or publishers, you may be able to obtain free advertising in exchange for your goods or services. What might be useful to the media? Free meals in restaurants for entertaining advertisers, free goods—vacations, admissions, merchandise—for use in promotional sweepstakes, printing, bookkeeping, cleaning, paper and office supplies and lots more. But before you get yourself what's known in the industry as a "trade-out deal," ask: Do you *want* to reach this station's or publication's audience with your message? Restaurants, stores and tourist attractions might answer "yes"—but if you own a janitorial or bookkeeping service, you're probably better off getting paid in real dollars and then investing them in some good business-to-business media.

3. ***Don't overlook small space ads.*** Small space ads and classified ads can be an inexpensive way of really boosting business. The key to these ads is so simple, but it's all-too-often overlooked: *Always have a strong offer—something too good to pass up*. These ads are not about creating an image. They're about creating sales, and to make that phone or doorbell ring, you'll need to provide a very significant reason to buy. Another tip: Use a device to create a sense of urgency, such as "First 100 callers also get a free watchamacallit" or "Offer good only through April 15th." A strong offer coupled with a message to "do it now" works wonders.

4. ***Yellow Pages ads can get great results—but don't overspend.*** The Yellow Pages is a fabulous marketing tool, because its users are usually ready to purchase. There are many ways to increase your Yellow Page ad's effectiveness and reduce your costs—enough, in fact, to fill a book: *Getting the Most from Your Yellow Pages Advertising,* by Barry Mahler, published by AMACOM Press. If you're spending a significant amount on Yellow Page advertising, we suggest you give it a read.

Some good ideas for the rest of us:

- *Know the alphabet.* Ever wonder why there are so many "AAA Printing Services" and "AAAA Locksmiths" in the Yellow Pages? The answer is simple: Since people usually start by reading the ads at the beginning of the listings, and then skim through, pausing at the bigger display ads, it's an advantage to be near the top of the listings. At the top of the listings, a smaller, in-column advertisement will have an impact similar to that of a more expensive display ad further down. OK, so your name is "Zebra Finishings?" You can gain an alphabetical advantage by registering a second "doing business as" (DBA) name that falls at the beginning of the alphabet, and getting a listing under this name.
- *Don't buy more space than you need to stand out.* You'll want an ad that's larger than the competition's—but it doesn't need to *dwarf* the competitors. One size larger will usually suffice.
- *Color can be a real stand out technique.* Most, if not all, Yellow Pages now allow listings in red. They'll charge you more for this—but color really makes your ad stand out, and it may be worth it. Of course, this game will change when all your competitors are also in color.
- *Be creative about listings.* How often have you, yourself, been searching for a specific product and have not been able to figure out the right heading to look under in the Yellow Pages? Chances are, your customers may have the same problems. You'll stand more chance of making a sale if you are listed under *all* the subjects that your customers could possibly be thinking about. For instance, if you sell a full line of shoes, boots and athletic shoes, you might want to consider small space listings (called "squints") under "Exercise Apparel," "Raingear," "Camping Equipment," and "Hiking Equipment." Squints are extremely inexpensive—and sometimes, you're the only competitor listed there! A tip: Ask your callers what listing they looked under and track the responses, so you can determine which additional listings are most effective.
- *If your competitors aren't advertising, maybe you shouldn't either.* Maybe your competitors are just missing the boat. But maybe they've tried to advertise, and it just hasn't worked. You can check this out very easily: Ask your customers if they considered using the Yel-

low Pages, or if they tried to do so. If not, maybe the Yellow Pages isn't for you.

- *Use offers in your copy.* "Mention this ad and get $X or X% off your first order" is a good one. Not only does it help set you apart from the competition, but it also aids you in tracking the effectiveness of your Yellow Pages advertising.

5. *Advertise on the Internet—for free.* The Internet is a loose network of tens of millions of users—a loose conglomeration of thousands of interest groups, user forums, lists, and newsgroups. Each group represents a sort of electronic "minicommunity" with its own interests, rules and history. Advertisers are looking closely at this new medium, because it allows targeted access to specific interest groups and *there's no charge (other than access fees and data inputting costs) to get the message out there.*

Is Cyberspace a marketer's Nirvana? Yes, in that it allows you practically free access to *targeted* groups of people who may be interested in your goods or services. But beware—you must approach this medium with a good deal of sensitivity and good sense, or you stand the risk of getting "flamed"—that is receiving all sorts of nasty messages from other 'Net users angered at your marketing techniques. To avoid upsetting the very people you want to attract, follow these tips:

- *Know the values and mores of the user forums you're targeting.* Some groups are far less tolerant of commercial messages than others. Listen in, and see what happens if someone leaves an advertising-like message. If the user gets "flamed," perhaps you should avoid commercialism with this group. Another way to understand the group's values is to contact the forum moderator and ask him or her.
- *Keep everything short and simple.* Keep the message to two screens (about 50 lines) or less. That way, it'll get read, and it won't be too long to annoy people who pay an access charge to get on the Internet.
- *Go for content, not for flash.* This is not the forum for lots of hype. It *is* the forum for a lot of useful information. Find a way to add value to your message, not advertiser-ese.
- *Target your postings.* Something that's automatically guaranteed to get you "flamed" is sending out something to a broad array of forums whose users have no interest in your products. Select the

user groups carefully on the basis of their potential need for your products or services.

6. ***Try broadcast fax for quick response.*** Broadcast fax—sending a faxed offer to a targeted list of potential buyers—can be a great way to quickly get the word out for business-to-business offers. Some tips on using this medium effectively:

- *Make sure you're sending the message to a specific person—not simply the "purchasing department" or the "Marketing VP."* Just like mail that's addressed to "Occupant," nonpersonalized faxes say, "junk mail." Don't cheapen your image or blunt your impact.
- *Provide a strong offer, and a rationale for using the fax.* "We're faxing you because we thought you'd want to know as soon as possible about this three-for-two offer—and because it's such a limited-time offer that we couldn't wait for the mail." That's the kind of message that works *with* the fax medium, not against it.
- *Test the fax's design for clarity before you send it.* Is it readable even when received on poor-quality fax machines? If not, redesign it. A typical mistake is adding in shading—it often renders things illegible.
- *Carefully design your faxable order form.* If you accept orders by fax, test the order form's design. Never shade anything you'll need to read, such as the client's address, telephone number, signature or credit card number. And try to avoid small-point or italic type—it breaks up.
- *Here's how to get the fax from your desk to their fax machine.* If it's a small batch, and you have a sophisticated fax machine that has broadcast capabilities built in, you can do it yourself. Remember to send these faxes at night, when phone rates are cheapest—and make sure that your fax machine has a 14,400 baud rate or better, to ensure fastest possible transmission. You also have the option of going outside to an independent fax broadcast service. Some of the "Baby Bells" and other long distance carriers offer this service.

7. ***Keep your production costs in hand.*** Production costs can be significant—it's not unusual to pay $15,000 or more for a television commercial, and artwork and separations for print ads can run into the hundreds, if not thousands. There are, however, things you can do to keep a lid on these costs.

- *For television productions, make decisions up front on what you'll be doing, and stick to them.* When you decide before you shoot *exactly* what shots you'll be taking, two things happen: Your agency can rent only the equipment it really needs, and you won't have to shoot loads of extra film to make sure that you haven't missed an angle or a nuance. As our resident production expert puts it, "The fat of production lies in indecision." If you work with your agency to carefully plan the shoot, you can save many thousands of dollars. A caveat: Don't complain if, on the day of the shoot, you decide you want something that can't be done with the available equipment. You give up a little flexibility in the interest of savings.

- *Be aware of the cost impact of production decisions.* Every decision you make regarding a production—the look, the feel, the location—has the potential to have a major effect on costs. For instance, if you shoot a commercial in 35 mm film, it will look more "finished"—but cost many thousands of dollars more than shooting on videotape. A black and white advertisement or brochure will be far less expensive to produce than a four-color one. Using stock footage or soundtracks will often be cheaper than creating them yourself. Shooting in a right-to-work state means you don't have to use expensive union labor—it might be worth airfare and lodging to do so. Using one fewer actor can often save you thousands on residuals. If you keep these things in mind, you can often find creative ways to reduce costs. At the very least, you'll be making an informed decision.

- *Have a freelance designer create print advertising "templates" so you can create ads in-house.* Have the designer create these templates in a variety of sizes and layouts, and then import them into your desktop publishing program. That way, you can change the copy yourself whenever you want to without interfering with your overall consistent, professional image.

- *Do some of the design work in-house.* With the advent of desktop publishing, you can create some great looking print ads, brochures, handouts and coupons right at your desk. The key is not to sacrifice design impact merely to save money. Make sure you're not violating some major design rules. (There are books and courses on this subject.) If you're convinced you have no design instinct, why not hire a freelance designer to do it? He or she usually is far less expensive than your agency.

Going Beyond Advertising

If you're looking to create awareness and communicate a corporate identity, traditional print and broadcast advertising isn't the only marketing tool you have at your disposal. There are lots of other great ideas, including brochures, useful little "doohickeys" with your logo on them, nontraditional advertising media and lots more. Some low-cost options that bring in the customers include:

1. *Nontraditional advertising media.* People are bombarded with advertising messages in mainstream media, such as TV, radio and print. Have you considered breaking through the clutter with these?

   - Shoppers (free newspapers with local distribution)
   - Val-Packs
   - Tethered "blimps" and balloons
   - Take-One boxes (providing information and special offers)
   - Audio and videotapes
   - Shopping bags and packaging
   - Testimonials from satisfied customers
   - Flyers
   - Postcards
   - Gift Certificates
   - Doorhangers
   - Statement stuffers
   - Ad reprints
   - In-store signage
   - Matchbooks
   - Phone hold marketing messages
   - Newsletters

   All of these are cost-effective, proven marketing tools that often go overlooked in the rush to use more "standard" advertising forms.

2. *Advertising specialty items can have quite an impact.* Advertising specialty items are things like pens, calendars, baseball caps, T-shirts, notepads, key chains—little gifts with your logo and address on them that open doors, are great relationship builders and serve as ongoing reminders. Everyone loves free gifts—particularly things they can really use—and that's why advertising specialty items can be great business builders. To get the most from this marketing tool, try to

choose something that the person will use every day, and doesn't necessarily have (or have enough of). It's terrific if you can find something that relates to your business or drives home the marketing message—like sending a baseball cap to your best customers with a cover letter saying, "Our hat's off to you for being such a great client." Finally, the item can be inexpensive, but it shouldn't be *cheap*. It should perform well and look good. We've included some low-cost suppliers of advertising specialty items in our "Sources" section at the end of this chapter.

3. ***Use preprinted specialty papers in conjunction with your desktop publishing capabilities for ultra-high-impact brochures.*** It used to be that you had to go to a printer and pay a *lot* to get a good four-color printing produced. But as high quality laser printers have proliferated, many small businesses are discovering they can use them to create high-impact brochures, expensive-looking stationery and eye-catching promotional materials for very little money. The secret? Using specialty papers that have been preprinted with colorful designs, photographs, and artwork. The end product looks as though it's been designed by a great graphic artist (it has!) and printed using an expensive four-color process (it has!). Only it costs only a fraction as much: no design costs, no printer's upcharges.

Another great thing about these papers: You can actually customize your message to different customers without incurring huge printing costs. Want to develop a brochure that focuses on just one portion of your product line? Input the specialized version into your computer, and then print it out on your laser printer. Voila! Instant targeted message.

Specialty paper companies offer a range of products: trifold brochures paper, business cards, stationery, folders, covers, certificates, forms and more. They also carry papers with innovative add-ons, such as peel-off labels, perforated tear-off cards, prescored Roladex cards and business cards, and metallic foils. So you can carry through your corporate identity in *every* aspect of your communications.

We provide a number of suppliers of specialty papers in the "Sources" section below.

Trade Show Tips

Trade shows can be a great source of business, because they attract buyers who have an interest in your products or services. On the other hand, it's easy for costs to get out of hand, once you add in travel and lodging, lost time in the office, entrance fees and the costs of the booth itself.

Are you spending too much? Experts say you are if your leads are costing you more than about $150 apiece. There are two ways to affect this ratio: Increase the number of leads, or decrease costs.

To increase the number of leads:

1. *Let more people know you'll be at the show before it starts.* Before they visit large trade shows, attendees generally make a mental list of the booths they want to visit, then fill in with browsing and "word of mouth"—as in, "Joe, you gotta stop by Clark Company's booth— they've got a live elephant!" The most cost-effective strategy is to get on that mental list. That way, you'll have a systematic way to attract qualified buyers with interest in your *products*—not the pyrotechnics of your display. Mail, fax, advertise, write letters, call—but get the word out that you'll be there.

2. *Make sure everyone knows where to find you.* Have someone stand at the entrance with maps or slip them under participants' hotel doors. Give your people buttons with your booth's number on them, and give visitors a little sticker or button with your booth's number on it, too.

3. *Use good sales techniques at the booth.* Listen. Don't sell too hard. Try to ascertain the visitor's needs. Invite conversation and give and take. You know all the right moves—just make sure that you and your people follow them. One other thing—arrange for a quiet, private "closing" area in your booth, where you can actually make the final deal.

4. *Have a good way of capturing leads and information.* At trade shows, you'll get hot leads—people who are ready to buy, and who require fast followup, medium leads—people who are interested but aren't yet at the purchase point, and warm/cool leads—people who are happy to drop their business cards in a fishbowl in the hopes they'll win a cruise to Tahiti. You need to develop a way to separate these leads and attack them with the right level of followup. In addition, you should devise a way to capture a significant amount of information about hot and medium leads, such as who else they're considering, when they'd like to buy, what they think about your products, and agreed-upon followup. Short information capture forms should do the trick.

5. *Arrange for enough peoplepower.* Experts say you'll need at least four

people to ensure enough coverage. It gets exhausting to be on your feet and "on" all day.

To decrease costs:

6. ***Consider buying a preowned booth.*** New booths are extremely expensive. If you're not proud, you can save 50–80% by purchasing used booths. We tell you where you can obtain these booths in the "Sources" section of this chapter.
7. ***Don't pay for services you can do yourself.*** Trade shows will do your vacuuming and cleaning for you—but the markup on these services is outrageous. It's cheaper to buy a light vacuum and some cleaning materials and ship it with the booth. A half-hour of your own elbow grease here and there will save you hundreds.
8. ***Think ahead to avoid expensive last-minute purchases.*** There are things you'll always need at a trade show: gaffer's tape, masking tape, shipping and packing supplies, extension cords, paper, clipboards, pencils/pens and the like. If you forget these and have to buy them on-site, you'll pay through the nose. To avoid this, make a checklist of everything you need, and bring it from the office.

There are many other ways to decrease costs and increase trade show impact. Skyline Displays, a major booth manufacturer, has put together a free, 50-page booklet, *The Trade Show Marketing Idea Kit,* that gives you cost-saving and impact-increasing tips and worksheets. To get it, contact Skyline Displays, 1301 East Cliff Road, Burnsville, MN 55337; 1-800-328-2725; fax: 1-612-895-6318.

Public Relations

Public relations can be even more powerful than advertising. Because PR is presented as "news," it is often perceived as being more credible than "advertising." The upshot? You'll spend less work convincing the audience you're telling the truth about the benefits of your products or services. Public relations is an entire discipline in and of itself, and we don't have time or space to fully explore it here. But there are a couple of ways you can get the most from your PR dollars:

1. ***Create a newsworthy story that is of interest to the publications you're targeting.*** Remember that different publications require different

slants. "Clark Co. introduces new plastics process" is great for a trade magazine, but "Clark Co. introduces new plastics process that means training and jobs for local residents" is far better for your local newspaper.

2. ***Clean up your news release mailing lists to increase effectiveness, reduce mailing costs.*** Have someone spend the time to confirm addresses and titles. Editors like to get letters addressed to them, not their predecessor. And it's helpful to have accurate addresses if you're sending time-sensitive material. Finally, you can save postage over and over if you eliminate unproductive or defunct publications.

3. ***The shorter the release, the better.*** If you don't grab the editor in the first two sentences, you're usually sunk. So don't send a long press release when a short one will do. Another benefit: Short releases are cheaper to reproduce and send.

4. ***Professionalism and a good story will win out over flash.*** A cleanly typed press release that has real news or human interest in it is usually all you need to start the ball rolling on press coverage. You don't need fancy stationery or elaborate artwork. Save your money for the important things, like . . .

5. ***Follow-up.*** To ensure placement of the really important stories in the key publications, call and talk to the editor. Remember, this is as much a sales call as one in which you're selling your product, only this time, you're selling an idea. Understand what the editor is looking for, and you'll be halfway home. And once an editor runs a story, do the courteous thing—call him or her and thank him for the coverage.

6. ***Once you have the press, use it and use it again.*** Reproduce the big stories and send them with a cover letter to customers and prospects. It's a good way to keep your name in front of your target market, and it can enhance their impression of your substance and credibility. And you might consider enlarging and displaying really positive press coverage in your reception or conference rooms.

We hope the preceding discussion has provided some direction for saving money on marketing without hurting the effectiveness of your efforts. On the next several pages, we provide some sources of marketing-related services and products.

SOURCES:

MARKETING, PROMOTION AND ADVERTISING

BEAVERPRINTS
Main Street
Bellwood, PA 16617

1-800-9-BEAVER (1-800-923-2837)

BeaverPrints focuses on preprinted brochures, although it also offers a limited selection of stationery and other papers. An innovative aspect of their product line: They offer preprinted brochures with four-color stock photography of people, industries and other subjects.

Outlet Type:	Catalog house.
Product Line:	Preprinted brochures, many designs using stock photography. Limited selection of matching stationery sets including letterhead, envelopes, cards, Roladex address cards and the like. Check out their "Business-in-a-Box" kits, which include letterhead, envelopes, cards, trifold brochures and presentation folders.
Fax:	1-800-BEAVER 4 (1-800-232-8374)
Information:	Catalog (free); sample kits ($39 and $89).
Orders Accepted By:	Mail, fax, phone.
Payment:	Visa, MasterCard, American Express; check or money order; COD ($5 additional charge); qualified companies can open an account (net 20 days).

Delivery:	No handling charges; shipping charges vary depending on size of order: $6.95 for orders under $200, free shipping for orders over $200. Fed Ex standard overnight available at extra charge (amount varies by size of order).
Guarantees:	Money back at any time if not satisfied.

THE EXHIBIT EMPORIUM

38503 Cherry Street
Newark, CA 94560

1-800-541-9100

The Exhibit Emporium buys and sells used trade show booths at a fraction of their original cost. Whether you're looking to trade up from your current booth, or to obtain a preowned booth at savings of up to 80% versus new ones, The Exhibit Emporium can help.

Outlet Type:	Catalog house, retailer.
Product Line:	Broad selection of preowned trade show booths, bought and sold.
Fax:	1-510-791-9115
Information:	Phone, brochures.
Orders Accepted By:	Phone, fax.
Payment:	American Express, Visa, MasterCard, company check, corporate account.
Delivery:	UPS ground service.
Guarantees:	30-day money back guarantee.

HIGHLANDER

1072 Jacoby Road
Akron, Ohio 44321

1-800-334-2230
1-216-666-6746 (in Ohio)

Highlander is a real specialty advertising specialist: It only offers items that have to do with golf—everything from tees to club cleaners to golf umbrellas to golf letter openers. They even offer a set of Three Stooges Golf Photographs not available anywhere else." Prices are good, too, and just get better as quantities go up. If you and your clients love golf, Highlander is a real find.

Outlet Type:	Catalog house.
Product Line:	Specialty advertising items focused on golf, including imprinted golf balls, tees, markers, divot tools, hats, towels, visors, umbrellas and capes, sweaters, shirts, gloves, golf bags. Note: Set-up charge for logos range from $10 for logos on wooden tees to $50 for logos on golf balls.
Fax:	1-216-666-4525
Information:	Catalog (free).
Orders Accepted By:	Phone, fax, mail.
Payment:	Check or money order in advance, Visa, MasterCard, American Express, Diners Club.
Delivery:	UPS. Usually 3–4 week delivery.
Guarantees:	None.

HUDSON ENVELOPE/JAM PAPER
111 Third Avenue
New York, NY 10003

212-473-6666

Hudson Envelope does not offer preprinted papers, but it does offer one of the broadest selections of specialty papers we've seen, with colors and sizes galore. And you can get excellent buys on their selection of closeout specialty papers. They also have a good selection of recycled papers.

Outlet Type:	Mail order; retailer.
Product Line:	Extremely broad line of colored stationery and envelopes (150 hues) and presentation folders (60

colors); excellent selection of close-out and "seconds." Recycled papers, specialty envelopes in a variety of colors and sizes.

Fax: 1-212-473-7300

Information: Sample kits, in-store, telephone.

Orders Accepted By: Mail, fax, phone.

Payment: Cash or check only at time of printing, although they plan to accept credit cards by Spring 1995.

Delivery: Shipping by UPS standard delivery. Fed Ex available at extra charge.

Guarantees: Money back at any time if not satisfied.

K-PRODUCTS
1520 Albany Place SE
Orange City, IA 51041-9987

1-800-369-2277

K-Products offers a variety of specialty promotion items, but its biggest draw has got to be its wide selection of caps. Seamless front styles, cordoroys, wool caps, mesh caps, hunting caps, Hawaiian profile caps—you name it, if there's a head for a hat, K-Products will fit it, and put your logo on it. Check out their other products, like their zippered jackets and vests.

Outlet Type: Catalog house.

Product Line: Specializes in large variety of printed caps (everything from embroidery, silk screening, embossing and everything in between). Also offers jackets, T-shirts, sweatshirts, golf and tennis shirts. Moderate selection of standard promotional items, such as address books, pens, calendars, clocks, key chains, bags, umbrellas, golf balls, cups and mugs, ice coolers, note cubes and memo pads. Note: If you don't have camera-ready art, they can create art for you for $35. There is a $10 per color PMS matching charge. Check extra charges before you place your order.

Fax:	1-712-737-8744
Information:	Catalog (free).
Orders Accepted By:	Phone, fax, mail.
Payment:	Check, money order, open company account (on approval after credit check) Visa, MasterCard, American Express.
Delivery:	Usually by UPS, added to bill. (They can tell you in advance what the charges are going to be.)
Guarantees:	Goods are guaranteed against damage only, e.g., if pocket is ripped or if seam isn't sewn properly.

MO' MONEY ASSOCIATES

P.O. Box 12591
Pensacola, FL 32574-2591

1-800-874-7681
1-800-346-0923 (in Florida)

Talk about a one-stop outlet! Mo'Money bills itself as "your total promotional headquarters," and it certainly lives up to its name! It's got the broadest selection of any of the advertising specialty suppliers we studied. Prices are competitive, and they have some interesting and unusual items.

Outlet Type:	Catalog house.
Product Line:	Umbrellas, sunglasses, headwear, ball caps, painter caps, carry bags, sportswear, shirts, sweaters, sweats, knit-ins, jackets, beach gear, dry storage holders, drinkware (plastic to ironware and everything in-between), scratch-off cards, back-printed tickets and coupons, stickers, flag products, small decals, cards, auto accessories, magnets, buttons, lapel pins, balls, balloons, key tags, luggage tags, lighters, golf balls, pens, stick note pads, clip caddies, clocks, calculators,

calendars, executive gifts, radios, edibles, more.
Note: Setup charges vary on each item.

Fax: 1-904-434-5645

Information: Catalog.

**Orders Accepted
By:** Phone, fax, mail.

Payment: Visa, MasterCard, check.

Delivery: 3–4 weeks, UPS ground service, Airborne or Fed
Ex, truck.

Extra Charges: None.

Guarantees: 100% return or replacement for items that don't
meet your specifications.

PAPER ACCESS
23 West 18th Street
New York, NY 10011

1-800-PAPER 01 (1-800-727-3701)
212-463-7035 (retail store)

Paper Access doesn't carry preprinted papers. But it does carry an extremely broad line of specialty unprinted paper, including over 100 styles of recycled stock. Check out their Paper Access kit ($25), which contains samples of their product line preserved in sheet protectors, keeping it orderly and clean.

Outlet Type: Catalog house; retail store (at address above).

Product Line: Broad line of unprinted specialty papers (over 500
to choose from). Particularly strong on recycled
papers, offering over 100 styles. Envelopes,
presentation folders, cover stock and more.

Fax: 212-924-7318

Information: Catalog (free), sample kit ($25).

**Orders Accepted
By:**   Mail, fax, phone, in store.

Payment: Visa, MasterCard, American Express, cash.

Delivery: Free by UPS ground service ($3.50 handling
                             charge added to each order); Fed Ex 1–2 day
                             service: $11.50 up to 20 lbs; Fed Ex standard
                             overnight $16.50 up to 20 lbs.

Guarantees: Money back if not satisfied.

PAPER DIRECT

P.O. Box 1514
Secaucus, NJ 07096-1514

1-800-A-PAPERS

Paper Direct was one of the first suppliers of specialty papers for desktop
printing, and has developed a very broad product line of well-designed
items. Not only do they offer preprinted stationery and paper products, but
they also carry a good selection of laser and ink-jet-compatible unprinted
papers (many with special coatings or embedded designs), presentation
products and overhead transparencies and handouts. Check out their "Pa-
perKit" and "PaperSelector" offerings; these provide samples of many of
their products at low cost (and they're free with a first order over $30).

Outlet Type: Catalog house.

Product Line: Preprinted stationery, brochures, presentation
                             materials; specialty laser/ink-jet papers; limited
                             presentation software and templates; limited
                             selection of related printing and presentation
                             equipment.

Fax: 1-201-271-9601

Information: Catalog, phone.

**Orders Accepted
By:**   Phone, mail, fax.

Payment: Credit cards (Visa, MasterCard, American Express,
                             Discover); pay by cash or check in advance;
                             qualified firms can set up an account (net 15 days).

Delivery:	Next day shipping available if order received before 3 PM Via UPS two-day service ($7). Next day standard FedEx ($8).
Guarantees:	Credit, exchange or refund if not satisfied.

PARKWAY BUSINESS PROMOTIONS
315 Fifth Avenue NW
New Brighton, MN 55112

1-800-562-1735

Parkway offers a variety of "traditional" advertising promotional items. We particularly like the fact that many of their promotional items—like pens, clocks, mugs, paperweights and printed pads—are great for the workplace. And that's where you want your logo to be top of mind. Parkway also offers a good selection of items for outside the workplace, too, and prices are competitive.

Outlet Type:	Catalog house.
Product Line:	Mugs and glassware, desk clocks, calculators, coasters, pens, lighters, highlighters, computer wrist rests and mouse pads, notepads, magnetic clip dispensers, paper clips, bookmarks, folders, leather goods (address, telephone, credit card holders, pocket planners), bags and packs, totes, sunglasses, stadium blankets and cushions, buttons, balloons, radios, stuffed bears, key chains, awards, golf stuff, flashlights, small tools and knives, sportswear. Setup charges vary by type of item.
Fax:	1-612-426-9292
Information:	Catalog (free).
Orders Accepted By:	Phone, fax, mail.
Payment:	Check, money order, corporate account, Visa, MasterCard, American Express.
Delivery:	Under 150 lbs. by UPS. Over 150 lbs. by motor freight.

Guarantees:	100% return guarantee. If for any reason you are not completely satisfied with any item, it will be replaced or your money refunded.

PREMIER PAPERS, INC.
P.O. Box 64785
St. Paul, MN 55164

1-800-843-0414
1-612-636-3602

Premier offers a limited selection of preprinted stationery and brochures. What it really excels at is its "action stationery"—a very broad line of preprinted letterhead with eye-catching artwork. Whether they're announcing news "hot off the press," congratulating employees for a job well done ("We've done it again!") or even admitting a mistake ("Oops!") these offerings can make your message stand out.

Outlet Type:	Catalog house.
Product Line:	Limited line of preprinted stationery and brochures; broad line of "action stationery" and matching window envelopes. Certificates and accessories, such as frames; banner rolls, limited software. Cards, some unprinted specialty paper.
Fax:	1-800-526-3029
Information:	Catalog (free); sample kit (free with first order over $30).
Orders Accepted By:	Mail, fax, phone.
Payment:	Visa, MasterCard, American Express, Discover, check or money order, COD, qualified companies can open an account.
Delivery:	Orders received by 3 PM Central Time will ship same day. UPS standard delivery (free with orders over $70); $5 handling fee for orders under $30; $6 handling fee for orders $30–70. Next day air available for additional charge.
Guarantees:	Money back if not satisfied.

QUEBLO (A DIVISION OF STATIONERY HOUSE, INC.)

1000 Florida Avenue
Hagerstown, MD 21741

1-800-523-9080

Queblo offers a good selection of preprinted papers that have been fully tested on laser printers and copiers. Designs are good; we particularly like their line of preprinted newsletter forms and foil-accented executive stationery sets. And their instructional books can help enhance your desktop publishing skills.

Outlet Type: Catalog house.

Product Line: Full line of stationery, awards, certificates, labels, including preprinted and blank laser, copier and offset papers. Preprinted templates for newsletters, scored and perforated papers, name tags, badges. Limited line of desktop equipment and accessories as well as a good selection of desktop publishing and word processing "how to" books.

Fax: 1-800-55-HURRY (1-800-554-8779)

Information: Catalog (free).

Orders Accepted By: Phone, mail, fax.

Payment: Visa, MasterCard, American Express, Optima, cash or check in advance, qualified customers may open an account.

Delivery: 24-hour shipping; orders received by 1 PM go out the same day. Via UPS two-day service. Fed Ex next day (extra charge). If you send a check with your order, Queblo pays the shipping charges.

Guarantees: Money back if not satisfied.

SALES GUIDES, INC.

4937 Otter Lake Road
St. Paul, MN 55110-9803

1-800-352-9899

Sales Guides offers a good selection of imprinted items, and a real benefit: free one-color imprint on all items. Another plus: They were particularly friendly to us over the phone—and this customer-orientation is carried out in their business, as they offer a clear, easy-to-read catalog and a "No Hassles" money-back guarantee if you're not completely satisfied.

Outlet Type:	Catalog house.
Product Line:	Mugs and glassware, caps, folios, clocks, picture frames, logo watches, calculators, ice coolers, coasters, pens, lighters, highlighters, notepads, sunglasses, belt buckles, magnetic clip dispensers, paper clips and bookmarks, folders, bags and packs, totes, sunglasses, stadium blankets and cushions, buttons, balloons, radios, leather goods (address and telephone, credit card, pocket planners), key chains, awards, flashlights, small tools and knives, sportswear, sweaters, tees, shirts, sweats, caps, hats, visors, patches, more.
Fax:	1-800-352-9501
Information:	Catalog (free).
Orders Accepted By:	Phone, fax, mail.
Payment:	Check, money order (additional 2% discount for prepayment), open company account, MasterCard, Visa, American Express.
Delivery:	Within 7–25 days by UPS where possible. Prepaid and added to invoice.
Guarantees:	100% satisfaction, or money back or product replaced.

WORLD EXHIBIT BROKERS, INC.

1507 South Wells Avenue
Suite 500
Reno, NV 89502

1-800-743-0330

World Exhibit Brokers buys and sells used trade show exhibits via a national network of affiliated trade show booth sellers. They're very picky about what they'll sell—they end up rejecting over 60% of the booths they're offered—and that means you can wind up with a terrific trade show booth at 25–40% of its original price. Another plus: They put their "merchandise" on a computer network that's linked to a Computer-Aided-Design ("CAD") program. So you can walk into one of their affiliated sellers, see on-screen what's available, and see how you might reconfigure it to meet your needs. Pretty slick.

Outlet Type:	Via network of affiliated trade show sellers.
Product Line:	Broad selection of preowned trade show booths, bought and sold.
Fax:	1-702-734-7500
Information:	Phone, at affiliated sellers' via computer.
Orders Accepted By:	In person.
Payment:	Company check.
Delivery:	Buyer arranges delivery.
Guarantees:	None. But World is rigorous in screening before it accepts booths for selling.

11

Office Supplies and Equipment

Copy paper, pens, file folders, paper clips, note pads . . . they may seem like small purchases at the time, but the money you spend each year on office supplies can really add up! Using the discount and wholesale sources in this chapter can save you 20–80% off the regular list prices of office supplies—even name brands. That can mean hundreds or even thousands of dollars more on your bottom line.

Good news: As the number of small businesses and home offices has grown, so have the number and type of discount and wholesale companies serving these markets. In this chapter, we discuss how and where to get the best bargains from four different kinds of sources:

1. *Catalog Houses* that allow you to purchase via telephone, fax or mail ordering, such as Quill or Viking;
2. *Warehouse Clubs* with strong office supply departments like Sam's and the Price Club;
3. *Office Superstores* such as Staples and Office Max.

We also include some:

4. *Light Office Equipment Discounters* that offer broad selection and excellent prices on everything from fax machines to cellular telephones to word processors and beyond, including 47 St. Photo and J&R Music World.

Each source has its advantages and drawbacks. Catalog houses offer good everyday prices and great specials. What's more, it's easy to use their catalogs to compare prices and shop around. If you're buying in bulk, their quantity discounts are hard to beat. Ordering is usually both easy and economical, because they generally offer toll-free telephone and fax numbers, low or no shipping charges, and shipping within 24 hours. However, you still have to wait for delivery, and you can't easily compare quality.

Warehouse stores usually have great prices on selected items. But it can be hit-or-miss: Sometimes they have exactly what you need, sometimes not. And they usually only carry one or two brands, so if you're particular about using a certain manufacturer, you might be out of luck.

Office superstores feature good prices, broad selection, and a chance to examine what you're buying. Plus, they're convenient: You can walk out of the store with what you need. Some even offer free next day delivery on phone-in orders. Drawbacks: They have more overhead to pay, so some of their prices can be slightly higher than other sources. And sometimes you'll miss out on some deep-discount loss-leader specials.

Light office equipment discounters offer a broader and deeper selection of equipment and electronics than most of the other sources we've included here, all at extremely competitive prices. If you're looking for a fax machine, copier, word processor, or other light electronic equipment—and you have a specific model or set of features in mind—they're a "must shop."

You can use one or all of these sources, depending on your needs and preferences. The rest of this chapter discusses the four different outlet types, tips on getting the most for your money when you shop them, and the best discount and wholesale sources in each of these channels.

Catalog Houses

Catalog houses offer one-stop shopping and a broad selection from which to choose. And these days, ordering from a catalog is certainly convenient: Just pick up the phone, send your fax, or even modem your order in—then wait for delivery in a couple of days. The sources we've collected here offer great discounts, too—ranging 20–80%. But you can save even more if you follow the tips below:

- *Order items in quantity.* Catalog houses usually offer significant volume discounts if you buy a lot of a certain item. If you know you're going to need it, you have the storage space and your cash flow permits you to make the larger outlay, buy more of an item. You can save 15–25% off the base price. Hint: If you really can't use enough to get the discount, try finding another business with which to split the order. Another hint: Even if they don't apparently offer a price break on quantity, ask for one—particularly if you need a huge quantity of something. They'll often negotiate one with you.

- *Ask for unadvertised specials.* Sometimes, the best buys don't make it into the catalog or circular. It never hurts to ask!
- *Place a large order—don't buy in dribs and drabs.* Not only is it more efficient for you, but it's also a way to save on shipping charges. Many of these suppliers offer free delivery—but only if you spend a minimum amount on the order.
- *Check "first-time customer" discounts.* If you've never ordered from a particular supplier before, be sure to ask if they offer an introductory discount. We've seen deals ranging from a flat $10 to 10% off a first order.
- *Get several suppliers' catalogs and compare.* Prices vary significantly; sometimes the lowest-priced copy paper supplier isn't at all competitive when it comes to pens and file folders. (Just see our Market Basket chart at the end of this chapter if you don't believe us!) It makes sense to comparison shop.
- *Check out house brands.* We were amazed at the difference in prices between national and private label brands for items such as correction fluid, transparent tape, address labels and copy paper—as much as 30–40%.
- *Watch out for big, thick catalogs.* Some catalog houses will send you a "full line" catalog in addition to monthly or bimonthly sales circulars. The full line book is great for seeing everything the discounter has to offer, but beware: Its prices often reflect straight list price or only moderate discounts. The big savings show up in the monthly and bimonthly sales circulars. Focus on these.
- *Be sure you're watching for specials in the catalogs.* Companies often offer "loss leaders" on popular items to encourage you to buy from them. Be a cherry-picker and save.
- *Check their guarantees.* Make sure they offer a money-back guarantee whereby they refund the purchase price if you're not satisfied with the merchandise. With catalog houses, check to see whether the guarantee extends to their paying the return freight—it should. And see if they offer a "lowest price" guarantee where they'll refund the difference

between their price and a lower-priced competitor. (Sometimes, they'll even add a further discount on the price!)

- *Use the information in catalogs to negotiate with local suppliers.* Before paying their asking prices, ask local suppliers if they can approach or match catalogers' prices. You can often negotiate good discounts, while still receiving same day delivery and dealing face-to-face with a real person.

Warehouse Clubs

Warehouse clubs, such as Price Club and Sam's, offer deep discounts off regular prices in a wide range of consumer and business merchandise. You can find some truly terrific deals on basic office supplies, computer supplies and software and office equipment. On the other hand, you may find these outlets less convenient than other sources, because you've got to go there and shop them—no mail order is available.

These outlets are truly "clubs"—you have to pay to join before they'll let you buy. (You do get one free visit.) Although you should call to find out each chain's specific requirements, here's the typical membership process: The first time you shop there, bring some form of identification that shows you own a small business—a company check, some letterhead from your stationery, a certificate of incorporation or some other form of documentation. Show this to their membership office, pay a small fee (this ranges from $25 to $45, depending on the chain, payable by cash or company check) and they'll issue you a membership card on the spot. From here on in, you'll need to bring your membership card every time you shop.

Is all this fuss worth it? Absolutely. Warehouse clubs offer some of the lowest prices we've *ever* seen on the core office basics, such as paper, pens and pencils, labels, files, clips, envelopes and the like. And we're talking name brand items here, such as Bic, Avery, Scotch and Pendaflex. If there's one near you, it's definitely worth a look-see.

But before rushing out and joining up, take note:

- *They're great for core business items, but not necessarily for specialty goods.* Warehouse clubs generally stock only the type of merchandise that's likely to turn over fast. That's wonderful if you're only looking for basics—for instance, if you're setting up an office from scratch. But if you need slightly more esoteric items, you're likely to be disappointed.

- *You can't predict what you'll find.* In fact, selection varies from day to day, week to week, and location to location, depending on the deals their buyers have been able to make with suppliers. Sometimes they only have black Rolling writers, sometimes only blue. The brands they carry vary as well, although they always feature one national brand or another. If you have a specific product and manufacturer in mind, you could be disappointed. On the other hand, sometimes you'll be in for a wonderful surprise bargain.
- *Be prepared to buy in bulk.* The goal of warehouse clubs is to move volume, so they make you buy a *lot* of whatever it is you're purchasing. Don't go if you want one pen or a single ream of paper.
- *They're not high-service places.* Warehouse stores are not the most convenient or service-oriented places to shop. They're generally located on lower-cost land, which means slightly out of the mainstream. Help is often scarce when it comes to assisting you in selecting merchandise. And they don't take phone, fax or mail orders or make deliveries. It's strictly cash/check/credit card and carry.

Office Superstores

Office superstores have really taken off over the last several years. It's not surprising—they offer businesses full-line selection, one-stop shopping, great discounts and lots of service. Many of them also have a catalog business, so even if you don't have an outlet near you, you can order through them.

Compared to other outlet types, office superstores' prices are competitive, although sometimes slightly higher than catalog houses' "specials" or warehouse clubs' everyday prices. (They're paying retail overhead, after all.) But although you may pay a couple of pennies more for some items (and sometimes you don't even have to do that!) these chains offer benefits:

- Great selection: full lines of products, with a variety of manufacturers represented.
- A chance to see, examine, and compare products.
- The opportunity to walk out with everything you need—no waiting for deliveries.
- Knowledgeable salespeople who can help you locate items and make informed comparisons.
- Free guaranteed next-day delivery.

Here are a couple of tips to help maximize your savings when shopping office superstores:

- *Join them!* Some of them give you extra savings on selected items when you become a "member." There's usually no fee to become a member.
- *Don't forget to check the house brands.* Although these stores certainly offer a broad range of name brand items, their cost of goods on house brands and private label merchandise is far lower. They pass those savings on to you.
- *Negotiate volume discounts.* Need a lot of a certain item? Don't be shy about asking the manager to give you a price break. He or she wants to move the goods.
- *Look for unadvertised specials.* Stop by occasionally to see what's on sale.
- *Buy from circulars.* These stores feature their loss-leaders in their promotional pieces. Read them and save.

Light Office Equipment Discounters

Light office equipment discounters are an excellent source for all the electronic equipment that a small business needs. Prices are extremely competitive; selection is both broad and deep, and sales staff is usually knowledgeable about the equipment. A number of tips to get the most out of this channel:

- *Check their service policies and warranties carefully.* Make sure you understand what's covered and where and how repairs will be made.
- *Be aware of "grey goods."* Grey goods are products that intended to be sold overseas, not in the U.S., and, for a variety of reasons, are priced significantly lower than comparable products sold in the U.S. Some wholesalers buy these cheaper goods overseas and then reimport them to the U.S. Then, they are sold at prices that seem "too good to be true." The catch is that these goods are not covered by U.S. warranties, so if anything goes wrong, you're out of luck. If you want to avoid grey goods, always ask if the product is covered by a U.S. warranty, and make the retailer put it in writing. And if you do decide to purchase grey goods, make sure that the retailer itself is willing to provide a warranty. (The ones we've included here do.) Another tip: Purchase

using a credit card, not cash; it will give you more recourse if the goods are "lemons."

- *Make sure you know what you're getting.* Although we've chosen sources with good reputations, the electronics retail industry does have some unscrupulous operators who perform a modified "bait and switch." The scam: They lure you in with a low price on one component—and then charge you double what you should be charged on the peripherals. You end up paying more than you should. Your defense against this scam: Get a total price on everything you need.

- *Don't buy the extended service plans.* Some electronics discounters offer an extended service plan that increases the length of the warranty. These plans make a lot of money for the retailer, and usually are not useful for you. (Our sources say you'd be better off putting the money you'd pay for one of these plans in a bank account and letting it compound—then using it if anything goes wrong!)

A final note: In this chapter, we've focused on commercial sources for discounts, but we also urge you not to overlook business and trade associations, which often arrange for their members to receive significant discounts on a variety of goods and services. For instance, the 300,000 members of the National Association for the Self-Employed (1-800-232-NASE, $72/year) receive additional discounts and special deals at selected catalog discounters and warehouse stores, as well as on a variety of goods and services such as rental cars, overnight delivery services, equipment and car leasing, business books and magazines, travel (5% cash rebate), and more.

We've told you *how* to buy, and *where* to buy, but we haven't told you *what* to buy. And even if you get the best deal on something, if it's a lemon you've still overpaid!

Luckily there are some terrific services out there that can help you make informed decisions about the best office equipment for you. These include:

- *What to Buy for Business,* a 10-yearly publication that provides comparisons and recommendations for everything from fax machines to phone systems to computers. Each issue focuses on a single product area. We used them in writing this book, and found them to be complete, unbiased (they don't accept advertising) and extremely helpful. *What to Buy* isn't cheap—a full subscription is $112 per year—but the good news is that you can buy single issues for $21 (buy two and get one free, too) so you can more inexpensively obtain those issues focused on the products you need to buy. Another information source published by these folks is *The Office Equipment Advisor* ($24.95), which helps small businesses decide what to buy and provides great tips on how to buy it intelligently. Contact What To Buy For Business, Inc., One Rebecca Lane, Pleasantville, NY 10570. Phone: 1-800-247-2185; fax 1-914-741-1367.

- Another source of purchasing advice is *UPDATE: The Executive Purchasing Advisory,* which is a monthly compendium of information and recommendations on products and services. Like *What to Buy,* it doesn't accept any advertising, and like *What to Buy,* it's not inexpensive at $95 per year. Good news is that you get a free problem-solving hotline with your subscription. Contact Buyers Laboratory, Inc., 20 Railroad Avenue, Hackensack, NJ 07601. Phone: 1-201-488-0404; fax 1-201-488-0461.

- An inexpensive source of great purchasing ideas comes from Quill Corp. (one of the sources we list below). Order *How to Save Money on Office Supplies* and for just $2 you'll get a 50-page booklet chock full of tips on how to save on specific products. Contact Quill Corp., 100 Schelter Road, Lincolnshire, IL 60069. Phone 1-708-634-4850; fax 1-708-634-5708.

On the next pages, we offer sources of discount office supplies and equipment.

SOURCES:

DISCOUNT OFFICE SUPPLIES AND EQUIPMENT

B.A. PARGH CO., INC.
P.O. Box 24510
Nashville, TN 37202-0918

1-800-BAP-1000

B.A. Pargh carries everything from adhesive to Xerox paper at wholesale prices. That means big savings for you, but there's a catch: Pargh is technically set up to sell to resellers, not to businesses that are end-users. Not to worry! Fill out their application. You may qualify, and if you do, you can "get it wholesale."

Outlet Type:	Catalog house.
Product Line:	Basic office supplies, broad range of electronic equipment, large selection of office furniture, basic computer software and supplies.
Fax:	1-800-247-4FAX (1-800-247-4329)
Information:	Catalog (free).
Orders Accepted By:	Phone, mail, fax.
Payment:	Open account billing on 30-day billing cycle for businesses with good credit history. You can also pay, in advance, by check or credit card (Visa, MasterCard). COD available.
Delivery:	No free delivery, but lower prices may warrant delivery cost.
Guarantees:	Money back within 30 days if product is defective.

BJ's Wholesale Club
1 Mercer Road
P.O. Box 9601
Natick, MA 01760

1-800-BJS-CLUB (for outlet near you—they don't take orders)

If you live on the East Coast, chances are there's a BJ's near you, as it boasts over 50 East Coast outlets, and is the largest chain of membership warehouse clubs in the northeastern United States. BJ's selection includes the best-selling brands in food and general merchandise. They believe in bringing in terrific merchandise for a limited time, and then moving on to the next item—so you never know what terrific bargain you're going to find. BJ's caters to the small businessperson and has a broad selection of office supplies and furnishings.

Outlet Type:	Wholesale warehouse club.
Product Line:	Office supply basics from large national manufacturers, office equipment such as telephones, fax machines, adding machines, answering machines, computers and printers, basic computer software and supplies, office furniture.
Fax:	Not applicable
Information:	In store only.
Orders Accepted By:	In store only.
Membership:	Anyone can join. Unlike the other wholesale stores, you don't have to own your own business or be a government employee. A $25 fee for one person, an additional $10 for a second person.
Payment:	They have their own credit card or you can purchase with cash, check, Discover Card. Stores have cash machines on premise.
Delivery:	None. Cash and carry only.
Guarantees:	Exchange or store credit if returned within 30 days with receipt.

47 St. Photo Inc.
455 Smith Street
Brooklyn, NY 11231

1-800-235-5016 (out of state or upstate NY)
1-800-221-7774 (in NY)
1-718-722-4750 (in NY or when busy)

Don't let their name fool you—if it's electronic, 47 St. Photo carries it or can get it fast and cheap. However, don't expect much help in making the choice, and be prepared for difficulties in getting through. O.K., so they're not known for their helpfulness, but they are well known for quality equipment and low prices. And they've been around for more than 25 years, so they must be doing something right.

Outlet Type:	Retailer, with some circulars.
Product Line:	Telephones and answering machines, cellular phones, two-way radios, pagers, fax machines, typewriters and word processors, electronic organizers, copiers, calculators, microcassette and dictating machines, vacuum cleaners, computers and peripherals, printers, software, as well as complete photo, video, small appliances, more.
Fax:	1-718-722-3510/11.
Information:	Phone, newspaper ads.
Orders Accepted By:	Phone, fax, mail, in store.
Payment:	Check in advance, corporate account, Visa, MasterCard, American Express, Discover, COD.
Delivery:	UPS. Next day Fed Ex or UPS available at extra charge.
Guarantees:	Satisfaction guaranteed; money refunded if merchandise returned, postage paid, within 30 days of purchase.

Fidelity Products
5601 International Parkway
Minneapolis, MN 55440-0155

1-800-328-3034

Fidelity offers discounts of up to 70% on a core group of office supplies, small electronics and stationery, and often offer great specials on brand name office basics. They guarantee fast, free delivery on orders over $25. If you're not satisfied, they'll give you your money back (except on software).

Outlet Type: Catalog house.

Product Line: Basic office supplies, some office equipment (calculators, labelers, laser printers), some office furniture (mostly chairs and desks), basic computer software and some specialty papers.

Fax: 1-800-842-2725

Information: Catalog (free).

**Orders Accepted
By:** Phone, mail, fax.

Payment: American Express, Visa, MasterCard, Discover, Diners Club.

Delivery: Free for orders over $25. Via UPS or Fed Ex (extra charge).

Guarantees: Money back within 30 days if not satisfied for any reason. You pay shipping and handling to return.

J&R Music World
59-50 Queens Midtown Expressway
Maspeth, NY 11378

1-800-221-8180 (out of state or upstate NY)
1-212-732-8600 (in NY)
1-718-714-3737 (in NY or when busy)

Although its name says "music world," J&R's name could just as easily be "electronic world." J&R offers great selection and deep discounts (up to 50%) on all sorts of things you need for your office. It's easily one of New York's best places to shop for light office equipment, and its catalog operation offers the same great discounts. (We shop there ourselves!)

Outlet Type: Catalog house, retailer.

Product Line: Copiers, calculators, cellular phones, telephones and answering machines, two-way radios, pagers, fax machines, typewriters and word processors, electronic organizers, microcassette and dictating equipment, computers and peripherals, printers, software, as well as complete line of the latest MIDI equipment for recording.

Fax:	1-718-497-1719.
Information:	Catalog (free).
Orders Accepted By:	Phone, fax, mail. In store at 23 Park Row, NYC.
Payment:	Check in advance, corporate account, Visa, MasterCard, American Express, Discover.
Delivery:	Usually via UPS.
Guarantees:	Satisfaction guaranteed; store credit if merchandise returned postage-prepaid within 30 days of purchase. No cash refunds.

LINCOLN CENTER BUSINESS MACHINES, INC.
111 West 68th Street
New York, NY 10023

1-212-787-9397

Lincoln stocks typewriters and typewriter supplies, as well as calculators, computer peripherals, word processors, fax machines and other electronics. They can save you up to 40% on machines by Brother, IBM, Minolta, Royal, Silver Reed, SCM and others. One big plus: They know how to service what they sell, and have a repair shop on premise. Another plus: They'll extend the manufacturer's warranties on some items. Note that their minimum order is $14.50.

Outlet Type:	Phone order; retailer.
Product Line:	Typewriters, word processors, fax machines, telephones, calculators, typewriter and word processor supplies and more.
Fax:	Not available.
Information:	Price quotes via telephone.

**Orders Accepted
By:**   Phone, mail, in store.

Payment: Check, money order, MasterCard, Visa.

Delivery: UPS.

Guarantees: Money back if item returned within 30 days.

MODERN SERVICE OFFICE SUPPLIES CO., INC.
134 East 16th Street
Los Angeles, Ca 90021

1-800-672-6767 (outside California)
213-748-4171 (in California)

MSOS is one of those finds that make life a pleasant surprise. MSOS competes very favorably with the other bigger names you might know and is lower on some products. They offers deep discounts on all office supplies. A plus for businesses in California, Nevada, Utah or Arizona: You get free delivery for orders over $45.

Outlet Type: Catalog house.

Product Line: Basic office supplies, limited selection of office
                             furniture.

Fax: 1-800-464-4171 [within California]

Information: Catalog (free).

**Orders Accepted
By:**   Phone, mail, fax.

Payment: Credit cards (Visa, MasterCard, American
                             Express); pay by cash or check in advance, open
                             account billing for businesses with a good credit
                             history, COD.

Delivery: Free to AZ, CA, NV, UT If order is over $45. For
                             orders from CO, ID, MT, NM, OR, WA there is
                             a charge of 8% of subtotal. For orders under $45
                             there is a charge of $3.78.

Guarantees: Money back within 30 days if not satisfied; postage
                             paid by them if returned in original packaging.

OFFICE DEPOT
2200 Old Germantown Road
Delray Beach, FL 33445

1-800-685-8800

Office Depot has over 300 stores at this writing, and is planning to grow to 800 over the next several years. It offers aisles and aisles of office supplies, furniture, small electronics—all the basics your business needs to function, and all at a discount. Call their toll-free number for the store nearest you, but if there isn't one, don't despair, because they also offer a catalog.

Outlet Type:	Office superstore; catalog house.
Product Line:	Broad line of office supplies, small electronic equipment (calculators, microcassettes), office furniture, basic computer software and supplies, office kitchen food (e.g., coffee).
Fax:	1-800-685-5010
Information:	Catalog (free); in store.
Orders Accepted By:	Phone, fax.
Payment:	Credit cards (Visa, MasterCard, American Express, Discover, Office Depot card), COD by cash or check.
Delivery:	If you're located near one of their stores, they'll deliver next day. Delivery is free if order is over $50 (over $200 for outlying areas). If you're not near one of their stores, they'll ship by UPS; you'll pay UPS directly for shipping. You can also place an order by phone and then pick up your order at the store.
Guarantees:	Money back within 30 days if not satisfied. They'll pick up for free or pay UPS shipping charges.

OFFICE MAX
P.O. Box 228070
Cleveland, OH 44122-8070

1-800-788-8080 (catalog order and store information)

Founded in 1988, Office Max has become a major discount office supply chain. The store has grown to over 328 stores in over 138 markets. They have everything from Apple Computers to paper clips, and publish a very comprehensive catalog, so you can order directly even if you aren't located close to one of their stores. Office Max guarantees the lowest prices on over 6000 items, and delivers free for orders over $50.

Outlet Type: Office superstore; catalog house.

Product Line: Broad line of office supplies, computers (both Apple and IBM clones), phones, faxes, furniture, software, peripherals, simple printed stationery.

Fax: 1-800-995-9644

Information: Catalog (free).

Orders Accepted By: Phone, mail, fax, in store.

Payment: Office Max credit card as well as Visa, MasterCard, American Express, Discover cards, pay by cash or check in advance (catalog).

Delivery: Free delivery for over $50. $12 if less than $50. Delivery is from the nearest store to you either by their truck or UPS.

Guarantees: Full money back guarantee if returned within 30 days of purchase. (Some stores offer a more liberal return policy—check!)

PENNY WISE OFFICE PRODUCTS

4350 Kenilworth Avenue
Edmonston, MD 20781

1-800-942-3311 (outside Washington, D.C. area)
1-301-699-1000 (within Washington, D.C. area)

Penny Wise can save you up to 70% on brand name basics every office needs, including basic office supplies, small electronics and stationery. Although they may not have the broadest selection, they often offer great specials on the core products you can't live without. They guarantee fast delivery, hassle-free returns on everything except software, and volume discounts.

Outlet Type: Catalog house.

Product Line: Basic office supplies, some small electronic
                        equipment (calculators, microcassettes), limited
                        selection of office furniture, basic computer
                        software and supplies, simple printed stationery,
                        some promotional premiums (cups, caps, key
                        chains).

Fax: 800-622-4411 [outside Washington, D.C. area],
                        301-277-6700 [within Washington, D.C. area]

Information: Catalog (free).

**Orders Accepted
By:**   Phone, mail, fax (24 hours), computer modem
                        (PC only). (They supply software, also available on
                        America On-Line.)

Payment: Credit cards (Visa, MasterCard, American
                        Express), pay by cash or check in advance, open
                        account billing for businesses with 5 or more
                        employees and good credit history. $10 off on first
                        order. COD under $100.

Delivery: UPS 2-day service. Next day Roadway Package
                        (extra charge).

Guarantees: Credit within 30 days if not satisfied; postage paid
                        by them if returned in original packaging; will
                        match any competitors' price if it appears in ad or
                        circular within 30 days of order.

PRICE/COSTCO

Headquarters:
10809 120th Avenue NE
Kirkland, WA 98033-9777

1-800-774-2678 (membership services—call for store near you)

One of the oldest and most successful warehouse clubs, the Price Club was
established in 1977 and merged with Costco in 1993. Today, Price/Costco
boasts over 200 outlets nationwide and serves over 16 million small busi-

ness members. They are strong on brand name office supply basics and can offer unbelievably low prices—sometimes as much as 70% off list prices. However, selection varies from week to week and location to location. Service is limited; they don't take phone orders or deliver, and in store help is hard to find. Be prepared to buy in quantity! You usually have to buy a lot of an item. Finally, you will have to pay a fee to become a member.

Outlet Type: Warehouse club.

Product Line: Office supply basics from large national manufacturers, office equipment such as telephones, fax machines, adding machines, answering machines, computers and printers, basic computer software and supplies, office furniture.

Fax: Not applicable.

Information: In store only.

**Orders Accepted
By:**   In store only.

Membership: A $25 fee for one person, an additional $10 for a second person. You need to show that you are a business owner with any three pieces of company ID: letterhead, business card, check, etc.

Payment: Cash, company check, Discover. Stores have cash machines on premise should you run short.

Delivery: None. Cash and carry only.

Guarantees: Exchange or store credit if returned within 30 days with receipt.

QUILL CORPORATION
100 Shelter Road
Lincolnshire, IL 60069-3621

1-708-634-4800

Quill is the grand old-timer in the direct mail office business and offers discounts of up to 81% (see their "Barnburner Specials"). They also offer deep discounts on small electronics and stationery. Quill provides fast, free delivery (Note: You must place a minimum order of $25), volume discounts, and no–questions–asked 30-day guarantees on everything except software.

Outlet Type:	Catalog house.
Product Line:	Basic office supplies, some small electronic equipment (calculators, microcassettes), limited selection of office furniture, simple printed stationery.
Fax:	1–708–634–5708
Information:	Catalog (free).
Orders Accepted By:	Phone, mail, fax.
Payment:	Set up an account by phone (terms: net 30), Credit cards (Visa, MasterCard). No COD.
Delivery:	Free if over $25 via UPS 2-day service. Fed Ex next day available at extra charge.
Guarantees:	Money back within 30–90 days if not satisfied (time limit depends on merchandise).

Reliable Corporation
1001 W. Van Buren Street
Chicago, IL 60680

1–800–869–6000

Reliable is a big player in the office supply game, and their size allows them to offer deep discounts on everything you'll need for your office, from supplies to equipment.

Outlet Type:	Catalog house.
Product Line:	Basic office supplies, some office equipment (calculators, stand alone word processors, shredders, etc.), some office furniture (mostly chairs, desks, files, and printer stands), some computer software and supplies.

Fax:	1-800-326-3233
Information:	Catalog (free).
Orders Accepted By:	Phone, mail, fax.
Payment:	American Express, Visa, MasterCard, Discover; house account if you have a good credit history. No COD.
Delivery:	$2.99 handling charge plus delivery charges, unless order is over $25 *and* it's an item stocked in their warehouses. For the latter orders, there's a handling charge of $1.28, but no shipping charges. Shipped by UPS.
Guarantees:	Money back within 30 days if not satisfied; postage paid by Reliable if returned in original packaging.

SAM'S CLUB

Headquarters:
c/o Wal-Mart Stores
702 Southwest 8th Street
Entonville, AR 72711-9078

1-800-444-SAMS (membership services—call for store near you)

This is the granddaddy of "warehouse" stores. Their 1993 merger with Pace has left them with 425 stores and well over 21 million club members throughout the country. Not only do they offer great savings on many brand name office supply basics and some office furniture and equipment, but also have a discount auto buying service, a travel club, a check-buying service (cheaper than your bank), as well as a very good buyer protection plan. As in all warehouse clubs, selection will vary from week to week and location to location. Know what you want because service is limited. Like other warehouse clubs, you'll have to pay an annual fee to be a member.

Outlet Type:	Warehouse club.
Product Line:	Office supply basics from large national manufacturers, limited amount of office equipment such as telephones, fax machines, adding machines,

answering machines, computers and printers, basic computer software and supplies, office furniture.

Fax: Not applicable.

Information: In store only.

**Orders Accepted
By:**   In store only.

Membership: A $25 fee for one person, an additional $10 for a second person. You need to show that you are a business owner with any three pieces of company ID: letterhead, business card, check, etc.

Payment: Cash, company check, Discover. Stores have cash machines on premise should you run short.

Delivery: None. Cash and carry only.

Guarantees: Exchange or store credit if returned within 30 days with receipt.

STAPLES, INC.
P.O. Box 9328
Framingham, MA 01701-9328

1-800-333-3330 (for store near you)

Staples, established in 1986, has outlets located in many states, but because they started on the East Coast, they tend to have more stores there. However, even if you're not located close to an outlet, don't despair—they also publish a catalog so you can order by phone or fax. Staples is certainly convenient—they'll deliver and they have just about everything the typical office needs under one roof. Plus, they offer good discounts—up to 50% off regular list prices—on a broad line of brand name, first-quality office supplies and equipment. Don't forget to become a Staples member—it allows you to receive discounts and take advantage of super special offerings in the stores.

Outlet Type: Office superstore, catalog house.

Product Line: Office supplies, paper, forms, janitorial products, mailing supplies, office equipment such as telephones, fax machines, copiers, answering machines, computers and some software.

Fax: 1-800-333-3199

Information: Catalog (free).

Orders Accepted By: Phone, mail, fax, in store.

Payment: Cash, check, money order, American Express, MasterCard, Visa, Discover, Staples charge. Minimum order is $15 with credit cards.

Delivery: Next day delivery available. Charges are 5% of the cost of your order, with a minimum delivery charge of $15.

Guarantees: Returns in original packaging are accepted within 90 days for exchange, refund or credit.

VIKING OFFICE PRODUCTS
13809 S. Figueroa Street/P.O. Box 61144
Los Angeles, Ca 90061-0144

1-800-248-6111

Viking is one of the biggest office supply catalog houses, and offers a very broad selection of office supplies and small electronics at excellent prices. They also have a limited selection of office furniture, computer software and computer peripherals. Of interest: Their line of promotional premiums on which they'll print your company's logo.

Outlet Type: Catalog house.

Product Line: Basic office supplies, some small electronic equipment (calculators, microcassettes), limited selection of office furniture, basic computer software and supplies, simple printed stationery, some promotional premiums (cups, caps, key chains).

Fax: 1-800-SNAPFAX (1-800-762-7329)

Information: Catalog (free).

Orders Accepted

By: Phone, mail, fax.

Payment: Credit cards (Visa, MasterCard, American Express); cash or check in advance; open account billing for businesses with 5 or more employees and good credit history. No COD.

Delivery: UPS 2-day service. Fed Ex next day (extra charge). Free delivery for orders over $25; under $25, shipping and handling charge of $2.83.

Guarantees: Money back within 30 days if not satisfied; postage paid by them if returned in original packaging; will match any competitors' price if it appears in ad or circular within 30 days of order.

12

Postage, Express Delivery and Shipping

Maybe because it's an expense that goes out in dribs and drabs—an invoice here, a package there, an occasional announcement to your customers, the once-or-twice-a-week overnight express letter—but postage, express delivery and shipping may seem like expenses that are too trivial to pay much attention to. Indeed, you may never have thought twice about these costs, unless you're a direct marketer mailing large volumes.

A quick back-of the-envelope calculation, however, suggests that it *is* worth focusing on. Think about it: Suppose you mail 100 invoices a month, pay 25 bills, and send out approximately 20 other letters a week, all at the basic first class rate of 29¢. Let's further posit that you send out two first class mailings per year to your entire customer and prospect list of 1500 names. Finally, let's assume that you're sending an overnight package per week at $13.50 each, and four or five parcel post packages a month. Add it all up—you're spending more than $2300 a year on postage, express delivery and shipping. And as rates keep creeping up, so do your costs. Just the price of doing business, you might think. No way— there are many ways to cut down on these costs. Let's turn to postage first.

Postage

Whether you're mailing millions, thousands or just hundreds of pieces per year, there are many easy steps you can take to save on postage.

The *first thing to do* is to contact one of the 70 Business Centers run by the U.S. Postal Service (for information, call the main post office in the largest city near you and ask for the number of the nearest Business Center). These Business Centers are set up to help small businesses with all their postal service issues, and they are terrific! Via pamphlets and seminars, they provide all sorts of free information on saving money on postage, building your business with direct mail and automating your postage and shipping capabilities. They even offer free on-site consultations (called "Operation Mail") where postage experts will visit your company to help you increase mail room efficiency. And a great boon: They'll clean and code your mailing list at no charge (see below for details).

Looking for other ways to save? Consider these:

- *Clean up your mailing list—for free!* At no charge to you, a U.S. Postal Service Business Center will clean your PC or word-processor-based mailing list, verifying and standardizing your addresses, eliminating undeliverables, and adding Zip+4 codes and carrier route coding. The result: faster delivery, ability to take advantage of Zip+4 and carrier route discounts, and less postage wasted on undeliverables. The process is easiest for MS-DOS or IBM-compatible users who can produce ASCII-format files on 3½" or 5¼" diskettes. However, if you're using a different system, the Postal Service can connect you with a vendor who can convert your files for a small fee. For more information, contact the United States Postal Service Business Center nearest you or Diskette Processing Services, National Address Information Center, 6060 Primacy Parkway, Suite 101, Memphis, TN 38188-0001. Telephone: 1-800-238-3150.
- *Get a postage scale.* How many times have you slapped on some extra postage just to make sure you've covered the cost? A postage scale can help you avoid paying too much: Savings can reach 10–20%, according to industry experts.
- *Get a postage chart from the USPS.* Postage charts are available for free from any post office. Coupled with the scale, they take the guesswork out of how much you owe.
- *Rent a postage meter.* Yes, a meter costs more than plain old-fashioned

stamps (about $18 per month for the cheapest version) but metered mail looks more professional and a postage meter can handle odd-amount (even fractional) postage. It's a real lifesaver when you have to send out a big mailing and a necessity if you want to take advantage of presorting and precoding discounts that result in fractional postage charges.

- *Keep odd-valued postage around.* If you *are* using stamps, make sure you have some non-29¢ ones around, so that you don't end up paying more than you need to for additional ounces. (Why pay 29¢ for an additional ounce, when the cost is 23¢?)
- *Use prestamped letters and post cards from the post office.* Strictly speaking, this won't help you save on postage. But it *will* save you the extra cost of the envelopes, because all you pay for is the postage.
- *Take advantage of USPS discounts.* The Postal Service offers significant discounts when you use Zip+4, bar coding and presorting. At this writing, here's what you could save:

	Savings on First Ounce
Zip+4	1.3¢
Presort by zip code (five digits)	3.4¢
Bar coding	.9¢
Total, 3 combined	**5.6¢ (almost 20%!)**

But before you grab at this bargain, consider: You must mail a minimum of 200, 250, 500 or 1000 pieces at a time to qualify for these discounts, and you must pay a $75 annual fee for each service. Finally, you have to prepare mail exactly to the USPS's specifications. All told, it only makes sense if you're mailing something in volume.

- *Go third class.* If you are sending a large, nontime-sensitive mailing, you might consider the biggest moneysaver of all: Third class (bulk) mail. The good news is that bulk mail rates range from 14.6¢ to 18.9¢ for up to 3.3 ounces. The bad news is that third class is perceived by many to be "junk" mail—and it may get tossed by the recipient before your message gets read.
- *Consider postcards.* Do you really need to send a letter, or will a postcard do? News of sales, followup reminders or notices of meetings or other events are often appropriate for postcards. It'll save you 10¢ per card, and your notice is likely to be read before it's tossed. Note: Your

postcard must meet U.S. Postal Service size and shape standards to qualify for the postcard rate.

Express Delivery

What in the world did we do before overnight delivery came along? It seems as though it's a ubiquitous aspect of business life. Unfortunately, it's also an expensive aspect: Sending just five overnight letters a month can cost you close to $1000 a year! Clearly, this is an expense category to watch closely. Some suggestions:

- *Make sure it really needs to be sent via express delivery.* Can it be faxed and followed up with a first class letter? Can it be sent for second day delivery? Are you sending it to ensure receipt at the other end (in which case, "return receipt requested" is as good, and much less expensive)?
- *Monitor usage.* Do some employees habitually let things go until the last minute, so that they have to "overnight it"? Do they use priority services when regular next day delivery will suffice? Focus on heavy users and wean them from deadline fighting and kneejerk use of the most expensive services.
- *Negotiate with your overnight carrier.* Overnight delivery services won't advertise this, but even if you're not a high-volume user of overnight delivery services, you can save 30% and more off "list" prices by negotiating a better deal. Federal Express is fabled for doing so; as we write this, it's possible for a company that sends only one item per day to qualify for a Federal Express Discount Priority rate of $10.85, down from $15.50, and a Standard Overnight rate of $8.35, down from $11.50. We provide contacts and procedures in the "Sources" section at the back of this chapter.
- *On Fridays, don't send something for Monday delivery by overnight.* Use the Postal Service's two-day delivery; it costs up to 65% less.
- *Don't use priority delivery when next day delivery will do.* Some carriers, notably Federal Express, offer two classes of service. Priority service guarantees delivery by 10:30 AM, whereas standard next day service offers midafternoon delivery. The trick is that many "standard" packages get delivered by 10:30 anyway. So ask yourself if the 30%+ premium for priority service is really worth it.

- *Best overnight mail bargain around: Express Mail from the U.S. Postal Service.* They have the cheapest published overnight rates, guaranteed delivery before noon, and a $2.90/2nd day/up-to-2-pounds deal that's terrific for less time-sensitive materials. (Note, however, that they don't *guarantee* two-day delivery—sometimes it will be delivered in three days.) There's no extra charge for weekend or holiday delivery (that can save you 30% or more)! Plus, unlike other carriers, they'll deliver to post office boxes. And just in case you're worried about the post office losing your packages, they also have free computerized tracking/tracing systems and full insurance. One caveat: They charge a $4.50 flat fee for pick up of any number of items, so if you're just mailing one or two things, it's best to drop it off at the post office or a designated Express Mail box.

Parcel Post and Packaging

This subject really breaks down into two areas: shipping *services* and shipping *materials*. Below are some tips on saving money on shipping services. We provide sources of discount packaging materials at the end of this chapter.

- Although smaller shippers abound, the two biggest ones are the Postal Service and United Parcel Service ("UPS"). The scuttlebutt we've heard: UPS is generally perceived as being faster, more reliable and, for most packages, cheaper. If you're making your decision solely on the basis of cost, here's a quick rule of thumb: Use UPS for everything *except* packages weighing less than 10 ounces and being sent less than 500 miles.
- If you'd like more precision in your decision, you can purchase simple software packages that can figure out the cheapest supplier. Two we've heard are simple and accurate are "Pony Express" for IBM-compatibles, and MacParcel for Macintosh users.
- If you're using the Postal Service and you only have one or two packages, drop them off yourself rather than pay the $4.50-per-visit pickup fee.
- UPS charges a flat weekly pickup fee of $5. So you should try to consolidate your shipments in one week.

SOURCES:

POSTAGE, EXPRESS DELIVERY AND SHIPPING

To Renegotiate Express Delivery Rates:

Carrier	Telephone Number	Process
• Federal Express	1-800-238-5355	They'll contact a Local Account Executive, who will call you.
• United Parcel Service (UPS)	Call local information or 1-800-555-1212 for the UPS service center nearest you.	Once you have the local number, call and ask for an Account Executive and tell them that you want to open or discuss your Shipper Account.
• Airborne Express	1-800-247-2676	The main 800 number will provide you with the number of your local Airborne Service Center. Call it and ask to speak to an Account Executive.
• DHL Worldwide Express	Call local information or 1-800-555-1212 for the DHL Service Center nearest you.	Ask to speak to an Account Executive.

Discount Sources of Shipping Materials

ARROW STAR DISCOUNT
3-1 Park Plaza, Dept. 93
Glen Head, NY 11545

1-800-645-2833

Arrow Star carries a variety of packaging materials, as well as other things for small factories: workbenches, dollies, steel storage, metal cages, etc. In addition, they have a very broad selection of storage items. Whether you have a small factory, or just a small business with packaging and storage needs, Arrow Star can meet your needs with discounts of 20% and more. And they'll meet or beat competitors' prices.

Outlet Type:	Catalog house.
Product Line:	Sealing tape and dispensers, bubble wrap, stretch film, shipping scales, poly bags, strapping systems, storage shelving, instrument carts, lifting and moving devices, pallet trucks, steel cages, filing and display systems, lockers, waste baskets, bulk containers, parts storage, shop workbenches, stools and chairs.
Fax:	1-800-835-2292
Information:	Catalog (free).
Orders Accepted By:	Phone, fax, mail.
Payment:	Check in advance, money order, Visa, MasterCard, American Express.
Delivery:	Shipping charges are FOB nearest shipping point (tailgate); for inside delivery there is an additional charge of $9.75. Usually shipped via UPS.
Guarantees:	One-year money-back guarantee. Also, if you see the same product somewhere else for a lower price they will beat price.

BROWNCOR INTERNATIONAL

400 South 5th Street
P.O. Box 04499
Milwaukee, WI 53204

1-800-327-2278

Whatever you need by way of shipping and packaging materials, Brown-Cor carries it, and at substantial savings of 20–40%. They offer significant volume discounts, so the more you buy, the more you'll save.

Outlet Type:	Catalog house.
Product Line:	Natural and synthetic rubber, acrylic, paper adhesive tapes, imprinted tapes, dispensers, boxes, cutters and knives, carton staplers, glue guns, mailers, staplers, mailing bags and tubes, soft pack wadding, loose-fill, foam peanuts, protective flow foam equipment, packing station, labeling machines and labels, shrink wrap, laminators, bubble wrap, stretch film, shipping scales, strapping systems, storage shelving, instrument carts, lifting and moving devices, pallet trucks, steel cages, filing and display systems, protective mats, lockers, waste baskets, bulk containers, parts storage.
Fax:	1-800-343-9228
Information:	Catalog (free).
Orders Accepted By:	Phone, fax, mail.
Payment:	Check in advance, money order, corporate account (after approval), Visa, MasterCard, American Express.
Delivery:	Shipping charges are FOB nearest shipping point (tailgate) for inside delivery there is an additional charge. Usually smaller items are shipped by UPS. Overnight shipping by UPS at additional charge.

Guarantees: 1-year warranty against manufacturing defects and workmanship. 45-day money-back guarantee if you are unhappy with your order for any reason.

CHISWICK TRADING, INC.
33 Union Avenue
Sudbury, MA 01776-2267

1-800-225-8708

Chiswick says that what sets them apart (aside from great prices) is their ability to evaluate your specific shipping needs and work with you to determine how you should set up and equip your shipping operations. Note: Although they've historically been focused on industrial users, they're releasing a "retail" oriented catalog that includes bags, ribbons, bows and gift boxes.

Outlet Type: Catalog house.

Product Line: Nylon and vinyl ties, sealing tape and dispensers, imprinted or plain corrugated boxes and cartons, strapping, bubble wrap, loose fill, stretch film, shipping scales, poly bags, mailing bags, waste basket liners, bulk containers, parts storage, hand trucks, advertising, mailing, warning labels. Some custom labels. New catalog will be released that includes shopping bags, ribbons, bows and gift boxes.

Fax: 1-800-638-9899

Information: Catalog (free).

**Orders Accepted
By:**   Phone, fax, mail.

Payment: Check in advance, money order, Visa, MasterCard, American Express, corporate account with approval.

Delivery: Usually ships by UPS ground service, but they can send by UPS overnight or 2 day air for additional charge.

Guarantees: Will refund or replace defective materials within
                         30 days.

FIDELITY PRODUCTS CO.
5601 International Parkway
P.O. Box 155
Minneapolis, MN 55440-0155

1-800-328-3034

Everything for the shipping and packing end of the business—that's what
Fidelity offers. Prices are excellent, selection broad, and their quantity discounts are an excellent deal. Another thing we particularly like: They'll
stand behind their products and offer you great guarantees, and will meet or
beat the competition's price.

Outlet Type: Catalog house.

Product Line: Packaging tapes and dispensers, imprinted tapes,
                         dispensers, corrugated shipping boxes, shipping
                         room organizers, cutters, carton staplers, glue guns,
                         mailers, staplers, mailing bags and tubes, poly bags,
                         labeling machines and labels, shrink wrap,
                         laminators, bubble wrap, stretch film, shipping
                         scales, storage shelving, instrument carts, filing and
                         display systems, protective mats, lockers, waste
                         baskets, bulk containers, parts storage.

Fax: 1-800-842-2725

Information: Catalog (free).

**Orders Accepted
By:**   Phone, fax, mail.

Payment: Check in advance, money order, Visa,
                         MasterCard, Diners Club, American Express,
                         Discover.

Delivery: In stock items are shipped within 24 hours and can
                         be shipped overnight by Fed Ex. Shipping charges
                         are FOB Minneapolis, MN They will determine

the shipping costs at the time you order and they guarantee to charge you only what you were quoted.

Guarantees: If you don't want it, they'll refund your money and pick it up at their expense. If it breaks within 1 year, they'll replace it at their expense. Also, if you see the same product somewhere else for a lower price, they will beat the price.

RAND MATERIALS HANDLING EQUIPMENT COMPANY, INC.
P.O. Box 3003
515 Narragansett Park Drive
Pawtucket, RI 02861

1-800-556-6468

Some of Rand's product line is really for the warehouse operator (do you really need a forklift?). But they also carry the basic shipping and packaging materials you need, and at a substantial discount versus "list"–30% or more. So even if you don't need a roller conveyer, they're worth calling.

Outlet Type: Catalog house.

Product Line: Adhesive sealing tapes, imprinted tapes, dispensers, boxes, cutters and knives, corrugated shipping boxes, carton staplers, roller conveyors, glue guns, mailers, staplers, mailing bags and tubes, poly bags, soft pack wadding, loose-fill, foam peanuts, protective flow foam equipment, packing station, labeling machines and labels, shrink wrap, laminators, bubble wrap, stretch film, shipping scales, poly bags, strapping systems, storage shelving, instrument carts, lifting and moving devices, pallet trucks, steel cages, filing and display systems, protective mats, lockers, waste baskets, bulk containers, parts storage.

Fax: 1-800-755-RAND (7263)

Information: Catalog (free).

Orders Accepted
By: Phone, fax, mail.

Payment: Check in advance, money order, Visa,
                             MasterCard, American Express.

Delivery: Shipping charges are FOB nearest shipping point
                             (tailgate); for inside delivery there is an additional
                             charge. Usually, smaller items are shipped by UPS.

Guarantees: Will replace defective materials with 30 days.

TIGERPAK
1037 Route 46 East
Clifton, NJ 07013

1-800-635-3851

TigerPak is a packaging and shipping specialist. Their catalog contains
nothing other than shipping and packaging supplies, and they offer significant discounts on most items. A nice plus are the books that pertain to
packaging and shipping. If you've ever needed to learn more, here's your
chance.

Outlet Type: Catalog house.

Product Line: Packaging tapes and dispensers, imprinted tapes,
                             dispensers, corrugated shipping boxes, packing
                             materials, cutters and knives, carton staplers, glue
                             guns, mailers, staplers, mailing bags and tubes, poly
                             bags, labeling machines and labels, shrink wrap,
                             bubble wrap, stretch film, shipping scales,
                             protective mats, waste baskets, parts storage, books
                             that pertain to packaging and shipping.

Fax: 1-201-773-5342

Information: Catalog (free).

Orders Accepted
By: Phone, fax, mail.

Payment: Check in advance, money order, Visa, Master
                             Card, COD.

Delivery: Usually ship via UPS ground service. Large items are shipped by truck. Shipping charges are FOB nearest shipping point (tailgate); for inside delivery there is an additional charge of $9.75.

Guarantees: 30-day return guarantee. If you are not happy with any Tigerpak product they will replace it or credit you.

Also see Office Supplies; many of the catalog houses and office superstores carry basic packaging and shipping materials.

13

Printing, Stationery, Business Forms and Specialty Papers

Stationery, business cards and sales materials *have* to look good. Often they create that crucial "first impression" about your company that can get your foot in the door . . . or have the door slammed in your face. But although your printed materials should *look* expensive and substantial, there's no need for them to *be* expensive—not if you use the sources we provide in this chapter.

Before we get into a discussion of what's available and where to get it, there are a number of key points to keep in mind to keep printing costs down and results good:

- **Print a lot at one time.** The major expense to the printer is setting up and cleaning up the press; additional copies cost only the paper and a little extra print time. That's why it pays to have a lot of copies printed. It's not unusual to be able to obtain 10–15 times the number of copies for about double the base cost.
- **Keep designs simple.** Art directors love to develop designs with four colors, bleeds, edge-to-edge printing, and nonstandard colors. All these things look great and can cost an arm and a leg. Make it clear to whoever designs your stationery that printing and production costs are important to you, and that you want innovative design without expensive printing requirements.

- *Make sure your designs reproduce.* Some logos just don't photocopy or fax well. (We know of one hapless sort who chose a nonreproducing blue for his logo!) Always photocopy and fax the suggested logos—then copy the photocopies and re-fax the fax. That way, you'll be able to see if the design can stand up to a couple of reprographic generations.

- *Have a two-tiered approach to printed materials.* By all means, show a fancy face to the client—but within your company, keep costs down by using a simplified, black and white version on internal stationery such as memo slips, fax cover sheets, and notepads.

- *Have "blank" business cards printed.* If you have a multicolored logo that's expensive to set up, have additional business cards printed without anyone's name on them. Then, when someone new joins the company, you can do a one-color press run and save yourself a bundle. Check with your printer to see whether you should leave these blanks uncut.

- *Savings on certain print colors are worth the wait.* Printers prefer to "batch" their color jobs, printing all of them on a single day, because it saves them clean up time and wasted paper. Often, they're willing to pass some of the savings on to you. Ask your printer if he or she will give you a discount for waiting until someone else is also printing in your color.

- *Proof early, proof often . . . and then proof again.* The most expensive thing you can do is not catch a typo before you go on press. The second most expensive thing you can do is to catch a typo at the last minute—you'll incur massive up-charges. The lessons? Always, always proof several times. Don't wait until the last minute to proof—make your changes as early as possible. Finally, have others look at it with a fresh eye—it's uncanny how a newcomer will be able to spot mistakes you've missed over and over again.

- *Check your paper assumptions.* You may not need to use such expensive paper stock. Or your printer may have something acceptable that's cheaper because he or she buys it in bulk.

The general tips outlined above can help reduce your costs no matter where you get your work printed. But there's another way to really reduce your printing charges: Use mail order printers.

Mail order printers take your order by phone, fax or mail and can turn it around for you in as little as a week. They can offer deep discounts (by our reckoning, 20–60%) because they buy paper in bulk, produce in volume and have no retail overhead. Most of the printers we've included supply stationery, business cards, forms, labels and more—although there are a couple who specialize only in one or two items. They're a great source for basic, noncomplex printing: one or two-color stationery, simple brochures, etc. But, with a few exceptions (see "Brown Print," below), we don't recommend them for more complicated work, four-color printing or jobs where you or a designer will want to go "on press" (that is, monitor the press run).

There are quite a few quality discount printers who provide their services directly, either by toll-free phone, mail or fax. Their prices are good, particularly if you order their "specials," saving up to 60% versus your local print shop. And it doesn't take long: If you select from their standard styles and papers, you can usually have your order within three to five days. (If you require custom work, such as inclusion of your own logo or two colors, it can take a little longer because you'll want to check some sort of proof before the final print run.)

You're not likely to have any problem getting a good price from these printers, and getting material within a short time frame. But if you've ever dealt with print shops before, you'll know that there *is* one major issue: getting back what you expect. Print jobs are usually full of surprises and miscommunications, and in this case, the problem is compounded because you're working with each other long distance. So before you reach for the phone to place your print order, read the following section to help you minimize the hassles.

If you ask the right questions and handle some of the pitfalls yourself, in advance, not only will you'll get everything you expect, but you'll save hundreds of dollars worth of lost time and aggravation. Here are a few things to help ensure savings:

- *Call a number of suppliers for catalogs, samples and swatches.* Choosing paper is a key decision, and it's something that really shouldn't be done over the phone or by looking at a photograph in a catalog. So, before you place your order, ask suppliers to send you samples and/or swatches of papers to be used for both texture and color. The are many types and colors of papers to choose from, smooth, bond, 100% rag, laid finishes, linen finishes, ivory, egg shell blue, beige, white, gray, etc.
- *Decide on flat (offset) or thermographed (raised) printing. Watch out here.* If you use laser printers in your office, thermography is probably not for you, because it will melt in the heat generated by the printer.
- *Try to order from one supplier.* It will give you more clout if something

goes wrong, and you may be able to save on the print run, particularly if you're using a special color. Plus, once you build up a history, they know your requirements and the look you're striving for.

- *Order by credit card where possible.* If something does go wrong, you can complain to your credit card company for a refund. They'll need proof of the mistake so . . .
- *Backup phone orders with a letter or fax* to the supplier confirming what you ordered. Request a return confirmation either by fax or letter. Keep *all correspondence* until you receive a satisfactory job.
- *Check their guarantees.* You have another fail-safe option if they offer a money-back guarantee whereby they refund the purchase price if you're not satisfied with the job.
- *Put together a spreadsheet that includes all the elements* and get quotes on the whole job from each potential supplier. That way, you can easily compare apples with apples and oranges with oranges.
- *Ask for unadvertised specials.* It never hurts to ask, and you may wind up with even more savings.
- *Be sure you're watching for specials in catalogs.* This is where the big savings come in.
- *Use the information in catalogs to negotiate with local suppliers.* Before paying their asking prices, ask local suppliers if they can approach or match catalogers' prices. You can often negotiate good discounts, while still receiving faster delivery and dealing face-to-face with a real person.

The points mentioned above cover *any* print order, from the very basic to the complex. But if you're asking the printer to do something special (e.g., a special design, or multiple-color work) please read on.

One Color (Custom Design)

A custom design includes your logo, or special fonts—or anything else that the printer doesn't offer as a standard format. If this is the case:

- *Layout everything just the way you want it.* You can even use a photocopy or a sketch of a logo.
- *Get a proof of the final rendering of the work from the printer*—as it's going to look when delivered. Note: It should show crop marks (i.e., where the paper is going to be cut or folded).

Two Color (Custom Design)

This is a custom design that uses two colors. This can be somewhat complicated, so:

- *Use a professional designer* whenever you can. They know what to expect. For every $100 of cost for a designer, you'll save $300 in time and frustration.
- *If you can't afford a designer* there are a few things you can do:
  - *Pick colors from a standard color matching system* that your printer uses. Most printers are familiar with Pantone Matching Systems (PMS).
  - *Ask printer if plates are paper, plastic or metal.* If your artwork contains two colors placed close to each other you'll need a printer who uses metal plates. Metal plates don't stretch with the heat of the printing press.
  - *Insist on a proof.* You'll want to see the work before it goes on press. And especially with two color work that is tightly-positioned or, in printers' terms, "has a tight register," make sure the proof is either cut where the crops marks are or cover the crop marks on the proof to make sure you like what you see.

This may take some managing and some agonizing the first time around, but it gets easier, and it certainly can save some money! Below we list the best discount and wholesale sources of direct catalog printers we've found, as well as sources of preprinted and continuous forms.

SOURCES:

PRINTING, STATIONERY, BUSINESS FORMS AND SPECIALTY PAPERS

BAP DIRECT

8500 Wyoming Avenue North
Minneapolis, MN 55445-1825

1-800-328-2179

BAP provides a full line of printed materials at good prices. They offer simple, clean designs, and a line of commonly-used business forms.

Outlet Type:	Catalog house.
Product Line:	Stationery, mailing labels, business cards, memo pads, printed purchase order books, invoices, envelopes, continuous forms, message labels. Custom logos are $15 per item (one time charge).
Fax:	1-800-328-0023
Information:	Catalog (free).
Orders Accepted By:	Phone, mail, fax (24 hours).
Payment:	Visa, MasterCard, free shipping with cash or check in advance.
Delivery:	7 working days on standard printed items from catalog. Ships via UPS 2-day service. Fed Ex next day, at extra charge.
Guarantees:	Unconditional money back within 60 days if not satisfied.

Brown Print & Co.
P.O. Box 935
Temple City, CA 91780

1-818-286-2106

Brown Print specializes in custom-designed business cards and stationery at up to a 40% discount—and you get personal service from the proprietor, too! Pat Brown has collected over 35,000 line drawings and says, "I can usually find someone something that works, saving them the cost of an artist." If you want something really special without paying an arm and a leg, you might check this out.

Outlet Type:	Mail order only.
Product Line:	Custom-designed business cards and stationery ranging from traditional to "different." Foils, foldovers, embossed designs, interesting use of colors and artwork are available.
Fax:	1-818-287-7307
Information:	Write for kit of actual samples and price sheet (cost: $2).
Orders Accepted By:	Telephone—he'll discuss what you want and then ask for artwork by mail.
Payment:	No credit cards. Payment by check only.
Delivery:	Normally 10 working days except for complicated orders.
Guarantees:	Work will be accurate, or it will be done over.

The Business Book
P.O. Box 8465
150 Kingswood Road
Mankato, MN 56001

1-800-558-0220

The Business Book offers a broad range of products and some very nice looking designs, with fast (six-day) turnaround and competitive prices. They also offer some signage and a limited line of office products.

Outlet Type:	Catalog house.
Product Line:	Stationery, mailing labels, product labels, business cards, memo pads, printed purchase order books, invoices, presentation folders, envelopes, continuous forms, checks, message labels, printed promotional items, limited number of signs and office products. Custom logos are $5 per item.
Fax:	1-800-833-1217
Information:	Catalog (free).
Orders Accepted By:	Phone, mail, fax (24 hours).
Payment:	Credit cards (Visa, MasterCard, American Express), pay by cash or check in advance.
Delivery:	Usually ships 6 working days from receipt of order on standard items. Ships via UPS 2-day service. Fed Ex next day (extra charge).
Guarantees:	Money back (including shipping charges) within 30 days.

DELUXE BUSINESS FORMS & SUPPLIES

3660 Victoria Street North
P.O. Box 64230
St. Paul, MN 55164-0230

1-800-328-0304

If you've ever written a check, chances are better than even that Deluxe printed it. Deluxe has been one of the nation's leading check printer for more than 75 years, serving banks and other financial institutions. But as times change, so has Deluxe. Today, it offers a full line of forms to meet your computerized accounting needs—a complete line of computer forms that are compatible with over 650 accounting software programs. Worth checking out.

Outlet Type:	Catalog house.
Product Line:	Computer-compatible checks and checking supplies (including those with customized logos),

accounting software-compatible forms (compatible with Computer Associates, CYMA, DAC, Great Plains, MAS 90, MBA, Microsoft, One-Write Plus, Open Systems, Pacioli, Peachtree, Quicken, Realworld, Softsync, Star, State of the Art, etc.), computerized tax forms, personalized forms and post-it notes, labels, stamps, organizers, business cards, stationery and computer printer supplies.

Fax: 1-800-336-1112

Information: Catalog.

Orders Accepted By: Phone, mail, fax.

Payment: Check, money order, American Express, MasterCard, Visa, Discover, corporate account.

Delivery: Shipped via UPS ground service (no extra charge for shipping). Overnight or 2nd day delivery available via Fed Ex at extra charge.

Guarantees: 100% satisfaction, or money back.

The Drawing Board

P.O. Box 620004
Hartford, CT 06101

1-800-527-9530

The Drawing Board offers an extremely broad product line and many styles—everything from stationery to greeting cards to printed purchase order books. We estimate you can save 30% or more, too, versus local customizing.

Outlet Type: Catalog house.

Product Line: Offers a broad variety of styles in many product categories, including stationery, mailing labels, business cards, memo pads, printed purchase order books, invoices, envelopes, continuous forms, message labels, greeting cards, presentation folders, screened binders, checks, custom forms, specialty papers, and office supplies; excellent design in a broad variety of styles. Custom logos $22.50 first time. $5 exact reprint per item (one-time charge).

Fax:	1–800–253–1838
Information:	Catalog (free).
Orders Accepted By:	Phone, mail, fax (24 hours).
Payment:	Visa, MasterCard, American Express, cash or check in advance.
Delivery:	Ships within 6 working days on standard items. Ships via UPS 2-day service.
Guarantees:	Money-back guarantee.

GRAYARC

Greenwoods Industrial Park
P.O. Box 2944
Hartford, CT 06104

1–800–562–5468

Grayarc's a good source for all types of forms—lots of different layouts and many different uses. They even have a separate catalog for computer and word-processor-compatible forms. And good news: You can save up to 50% off list prices.

Outlet Type:	Catalog house.
Product Line:	Broad selection of forms. Some small electronics (e.g., calculators). Some custom printing and stationery.
Fax:	1–800–292–4729
Information:	Via catalog. Specify whether you want "general supplies" or "computer form" catalog. *Include make and model of your computer or word processor with your request for catalog.*
Orders Accepted By:	Telephone, mail, fax.

Payment: American Express, MasterCard, Visa, money
                      order, check.

Delivery: UPS ground service. Next day delivery available at
                      extra charge.

Guarantees: Satisfaction guaranteed; return goods within 30
                      days for full refund.

McBEE SYSTEMS

P.O. Box 741
Athens, OH 45701-9980

1-800-526-1272

McBee is a forms specialist, offering a broad and deep selection of business
forms, especially computer forms and checks and other types of continuous
forms. You'll get simple, straightforward designs here; don't expect a
wildly artistic approach. However, the forms are very clean-looking and
functional. Another plus: Turnaround is fast—they'll ship two to three days
on standard printed items.

Outlet Type: Catalog house.

Product Line: Computer forms and checks, purchase order
                      books, invoices, and continuous forms. Also
                      provides limited selection of stationery, mailing
                      labels, business cards, memo pads, message labels,
                      custom forms. Custom logos: $10 first time charge.

Fax: 1-614-593-8288

Information: Catalog (free).

**Orders Accepted
By:**   Phone, mail, fax (24 hours).

Payment: Pay by cash or check in advance.

Delivery: Turnaround is 2–3 working days on standard
                      printed items. They ship via UPS.

Guarantees: Money back within 30 days if not satisfied.

MOORE BUSINESS PRODUCTS

P.O. Box 5000
Vernon Hills, IL 60061

1-800-323-6230

Moore offers well-designed and attractive letterhead, mailing labels and other corporate identity items, as well as a large selection of business forms, including computer forms and checks. Prices are very competitive, and they offer fast (three-day) turnaround on standard items.

Outlet Type:	Catalog house.
Product Line:	Limited number of letterheads, mailing labels, business cards, memo pads, but what they have appears very well designed and attractive. Large selection of business forms, (especially computer forms and checks) as well as purchase order books, invoices, envelopes, continuous forms. Some message labels, greeting cards, custom forms, and some specialty papers and office supplies. Custom logos: $25 first time per item. $5 log charge per item on reorders.
Fax:	1-800-329-6667
Information:	Catalog (free).
Orders Accepted By:	Phone, mail, fax (24 hours).
Payment:	Visa, MasterCard, American Express, cash or check in advance.
Delivery:	Usually ships standard catalog items within 3 days. 7 days on custom items Ships via UPS 3–5 day service. Fed Ex next day available at extra charge.
Guarantees:	Money back within 30 days if not satisfied.

RAPIDFORMS

301 Grove Road
Thorofare, NJ 08086-9499

1-800-257-8354

As the name suggests, Rapidforms specializes in predesigned forms. But they also offer other printed items, with straightforward, utilitarian designs. The prices are very good—we estimate you'll save 30% or more.

Outlet Type: Catalog house.

Product Line: Predesigned forms, mailing labels, business cards, memo pads, greeting cards, and custom forms. Straightforward, utilitarian designs. Customized logos: $20 first time, and $5 exact reprint per item (one-time charge).

Fax: 1–800–451–8113

Information: Catalog (free).

Orders Accepted By: Phone, mail, fax (24 hours).

Payment: Visa, MasterCard, American Express, cash or check in advance.

Delivery: They ship 4–6 working days on standard printed items, and ship via UPS 2-day service. Fed Ex next day is available at extra charge.

Guarantees: Unconditional money-back guarantee within 30 days if not satisfied.

THE STATIONERY HOUSE
1000 Florida Avenue
Hagerstown, MD 21741

1–800–638–3033

If you're looking for stand-out designs that really look "rich," The Stationery House is a good choice, because they specialize in specialty printing, including blind embossing and foil stamping, and they offer strong design capabilities. They also offer a full line of other printed materials.

Outlet Type: Catalog house.

Product Line: Specialty printing (blind embossing, foil stamping). Excellent designs. Also offers stationery, mailing labels, business cards, memo pads, printed purchase order books, invoices, envelopes, continuous forms, message labels, greeting cards, certificates, presentation folders, screened binders. Custom logos $12.50 *per item* (one time charge). Reorders: $3.

Fax: 1-800-55-HURRY (1-800-554-8779)

Information: Catalog (free).

Orders Accepted By: Phone, mail, fax (24 hours).

Payment: Visa, MasterCard, American Express, Diners Club, Carte Blanche, Optima, cash or check in advance.

Delivery: Ship within 5 working days on printed items via UPS 2-day service. Fed Ex next day (extra charge).

Guarantees: Money back within 30 days if not satisfied.

Also see:

- Viking Office Products ("Office Supplies").
- Chapter 1, "Banking" for check printing.
- Chapter 10, "Marketing" for specialty papers.

14

Travel

If you're selling, consulting or exhibiting, you or your employees may be spending as much time on the road as at a desk. So finding ways to keep travel costs down can be critically important.

Yet it seems that business people get the short end of the stick when it comes to travel savings. Take airfares. It's difficult for you to take advantage of the book-ahead, no-change-in-travel-permitted discounted airfares when you need the flexibility to change plans at the last moment. And those tickets that require a Saturday night stay? Forget it—if you've been on the road all week, the last thing you want to do is to spend a weekend in a strange town by yourself just to save a few bucks.

Lodging is another expense where business travelers seem to pay a premium. After all, tourists can find great package deals where they're paying just a fraction of the "list price" for their rooms. And unlike you, they can *plan* to take advantage of off-season rates and special weekend deals.

Business people just don't seem to get any breaks, right?

Wrong.

Businesses can take advantage of many ways to save on travel. But even if you don't want to do anything "special," you can still take steps to keep travel costs down. Some tips:

Find a Great Travel Agency That Specializes in Corporate Travel and Is Set Up to Save

Treat this decision carefully; it is the most important cost-saving decision you will make in the travel arena and can save you many thousands of dollars over time. It's worth the time it takes to meet with and interview a number of travel agencies. Apart from good "chemistry" and intelligence, look for a travel agent who's a member of the American Society of Travel Agents ("ASTA"). Also, an agent who is a Certified Travel Counselor ("CTC") is preferable; a CTC has at least five years of experience and has passed a series of difficult examinations developed by the Institute of Certified Travel Agents ("ICTA"). For a list of certified travel agents in your area, call 1-800-542-4282.

In addition, it's best if the agent:

- *Has a thriving corporate business.* An agent who understands the needs of the business traveler and is aware of the special deals offered to business people is key for good service and savings. These agents also have buying power with suppliers, so they are privy to special rates and other deals.
- *Is willing to work with you to keep expenses low.* You need to find a travel agent that is set up to help you save. Some things to look for:
  - They work with consolidators to get truly cut-price tickets (see Consolidator discussion, below), or they have access to tour fares and other special deals.
  - They belong to a consortium or hotel-booking service to obtain preferred corporate rates at home and abroad. (These preferred rates can save you 10–40% off the "rack rate"!)
  - They are willing and able to document the savings they provide.
  - They are sometimes willing to talk about rebating a portion of their commission on all or some fares.

- *Has systems to ensure you get the lowest fares.* At the very least, you want the agency to have a computer program that automatically ranks flights by cost. Some agencies get even fancier: Their programs book you on the lowest-priced available flight, wait-list you on cheaper-but-sold-out flights, and automatically switch your booking if a cheap seat becomes available.
- *Has a 24-hour 800 number.* Business travelers' plans change; flights get canceled or overbooked. You need a 24-hour-a-day source to quickly find you the least expensive replacement seat.
- *Subscribes to more than one Computerized Reservation Systems ("CRS")* e.g., Sabre, PARS, Worldspan, System One. Many agencies subscribe to only one reservation system. But by subscribing to multiple CRS, the travel agent can obtain better access to second tier airlines that may only participate in one public CRS; get earliest possible notice on seats

that open up; and ensure fastest access to the low, "fill this seat at any cost" fares that sometimes become available at the last moment.

Don't Forget Back-to-Back Ticketing

Back-to-back ticketing is a clever (but frowned-upon) maneuver that allows you to take advantage of the much lower fares offered for Saturday night stayovers. It works like this: You buy two sets of round-trip tickets with a Saturday night stay. One set originates in your city, and one set originates in your destination city on the date you wish to return home. You use the outbound ticket from the set that originates in your hometown to get to your destination, and the outbound ticket from the set that originates in your destination city to come home. Then (unless you can use them) you throw out the "return" trips from each set. Even buying two round-trip airfares, this ploy can save hundreds of dollars. But note: Airlines hate these tricks, and can give you a hard time about them. Your travel agent may be somewhat reluctant to book them, too, particularly if he or she is trying to maintain a strong relationship with the carrier.

Skip the On-Line Travel Services

There are lots of reasons *not* to "do it yourself" when it comes to making travel arrangements. The first is wasted time. Most Computerized Reservation Systems are complex and user-unfriendly. Fare structures are almost incomprehensible as well. Result: It can take you hours to complete even a simple transaction. The second is less chance for cost-savings. A good portion of the discount travel sources aren't yet listed, so you won't have access to many of the best deals. Also, as an inexperienced user, you may make a costly mistake or miss a big cost-saving opportunity. Finally, adding insult to injury, you may even have to pay on-line costs or subscription charges to use these services. The only good thing about going on-line is that it lets you see if your travel agency is getting you the lowest costs. But if you're worried about that, why not just bid out a trip to another travel agency and see who's cheapest?

Make Sure the Trip Is Absolutely Necessary

Can the business be accomplished by fax, conference call, letter, or video-tape? Can someone local do it for you? Business trips are extremely expensive, not only because of the out-of-pocket expenses, but also because they take you and your people out of the office, limiting productivity and availability.

Put Good Tracking and Monitoring Systems in Place

As we mentioned above, your agency should be able to document how much it saves you by showing you comparison prices on every purchase. And you should also track your employees to ensure that they're trying to keep costs down. (Did you know, for instance, that a common reason employees choose a more expensive airfare is that they belong to the frequent flyer program?)

Doing Business Overseas? Uncle Sam Can Provide Low-Cost Short-Term Office Space

The U.S. Department of Commerce's Export Development department will provide you with temporary office space at a nominal fee. They'll also provide translation assistance and local market information. Contact the Office of Event Management, Event Management Division, International Trade Administration, Department of Commerce, Room 2111, Washington, D.C. 20230; telephone 1-202-377-2741.

If You Do Business in Europe, Make Sure to Get Your VAT Refund

If you are *traveling* to Europe to do business, you are eligible for partial or full refunds on the huge Value-Added Taxes ("VATs") European governments slap on everything from meals to rental cars to hotels to gasoline to supplies. (You'll even pay VAT on trade show fees and training courses!) Since VATs can range up to 18.5%, refunds can be substantial. To get a refund, you'll need to obtain VAT invoices from the European companies who have sold you goods or services; these include the name and address of the U.S. firm, the supplier's VAT number, the amount and rate of the VAT, and the total bill including VAT. Then you submit this, along with a VAT refund request form, to the government for reimbursement. (European suppliers who do business with visitors from abroad are accustomed to the process and can walk you through it. So can the concierge at your hotel.)

Take Steps to Keep Car Rental Costs Down

Never assume you have to pay the quoted rates for car rentals. There are lots of ways to cut costs:

- *Negotiate a corporate car rental rate,* which is typically 15–30% lower than the "list" prices, depending on the amount of volume you'll be providing. Begin the process of obtaining these rates by calling the following numbers. (Please note that some of these are corporate offices, and are therefore open only on weekdays.)

Alamo	1-800-445-5664
Avis	1-800-222-AVIS
Budget	1-800-527-0700
Dollar	1-800-800-0088
Hertz	1-800-654-3131
National	1-800-367-6767
Thrifty	1-800-367-2277

- *Negotiate at the car rental counter.* In some car rental agencies, managers have a significant amount of rate-setting discretion. If they have an oversupply of cars that they need to move out, managers can be flexible on rates and/or upgrades.

- *Check out the car rental discounts offered by some of the groups you belong to.* The AAA offers deep discounts at major car rental agencies, as do several of the credit card companies. Professional groups (e.g., the A.M.A. or the A.B.A.) also have negotiated good rates. If you have an American Express Corporate Card, you are guaranteed 15% off car rentals at Avis, Budget, National and Thrifty.
- *Check with your car insurance agent and your charge card company to see if you're covered for collision when you rent a car.* If so, you can avoid the extra charges on their collision insurance with no worries.
- *Look at the refueling policy.* If they want a full tank when you return the car, fill it yourself; refueling charges are outrageously high.
- *Always have your travel agent compare car rental rates.* There can be a big difference between otherwise comparable services. Also, check out local independent car rental companies in cities where you often travel. Their rates are usually much lower, and the service can be more personalized.
- *Have the agent check out special promotional programs for car rentals, or watch the ads in the Sunday travel section of your newspaper yourself.* Some deals are better if you book them in your home town through a travel agent. And if you're calling yourself to take advantage of a special, quote the advertised discount and the promotion's discount code, as reservation clerks often won't volunteer the best price.
- *Check out the deals for weekend or week-long rentals.* Sometimes, renting for a week is cheaper than renting for a couple of days. And if you need a rental car anytime from Thursday afternoon through Monday evening, ask about weekend package deals. Weekend rates often start on Thursday now, and they can be far cheaper than ordinary weekday rates.
- *Give employees a wallet-sized list of corporate car rental and hotel discounts and how to take advantage of them.* Leave space on the back for their frequent flyer numbers, and they'll be sure to carry it with them.
- *Skip the car rental altogether.* Do you really need the expense of a rental car? Maybe not. For trips where you're simply going from the airport to the hotel and back again, many hotels offer a complimentary limo or van service. And even if you're headed elsewhere, don't forget alternative transportation—bus, van and especially rapid transit (rail/subway) systems. The latter are always cheaper, and often faster, than automotive transport. Atlanta, Chicago, Philadelphia and Boston all have good rail systems linking downtown with the airport.

Take Steps to Reduce Lodging Costs

Competition is fierce in the lodging business; there's over-capacity every-where. That gives you great leverage to negotiate better rates with hotels and motels. Some suggestions:

- *Consolidate all your business in one hotel per city, or in one national chain.* Use this as leverage to ensure lowest rate/highest service. Make sure your employees know about the discount and book there.
- *Always request the "corporate rate" when making a hotel reservation.* You can save 20% or more.
- *Use a travel agency that gives you access to a preferred rates program.* Typical preferred rates savings run 10–40% off list rates. You can obtain preferred rates through big multioffice chain agencies such as American Express or Carlson, by joining a travel club, or by using your travel agent—*if* he or she is a member of a preferred rate consortium or uses preferred-rate suppliers. Ask if your travel agent is a member of Hickory, U.S. Travel or Woodside, or if the agency uses preferred-rate suppliers such as ABC Corporate Services or Travelgraphics. (If not, we suggest you investigate using another travel agent. You're probably paying too much for hotels!)
- *At the front desk, never assume you're going to be stuck paying the "rack rate" in any hotel, even if it's what they quoted you over the phone.* If you inquire when checking in, they might be able to offer you a better rate or an upgrade unless they're 100% full. Another tip: If you're checking in late in the day, without reservations, and the hotel isn't full, you have greater leverage to negotiate a lower rate. After all, hotel rooms are "perishable"—if no one sleeps in the room that night, the hotel gets no revenue at all.
- *Join "frequent guest" programs.* The ones that provide airline mileage as well as free overnight stays are particularly good deals, and include:

Hyatt Gold Passport	1-800-544-9288
Hilton Honors	1-800-445-8667
Marriott Honored Guest	1-800-228-9290 or 1-800-648-8024

- *Check out the preferred guest programs offered by your charge card companies.* American Express Gold, Platinum and Corporate cards, for example, have negotiated preferred rates and other "extras" with a number of hotels in the U.S. and abroad. Other charge cards also offer good hotel deals to their traveling cardholders.

Join *Every* Frequent Flyer/Frequent Stayer Program—but Concentrate on One or Two

You should definitely try to concentrate your business in one or two airlines or hotels, but if you do a lot of traveling, it makes sense to join every program just so you won't miss out on credits during those times you can't fly your preferred carrier. After all, joining is free, and you generally get a hefty sign-up bonus. A few tips to make sure you make the most of your membership:

- *Don't bother taking the plastic cards with your account numbers with you when you travel.* They get bulky and you always end up without the club number your need. Instead, keep a list of account numbers in your date book, address book, or wallet. That way, you'll always have them handy.
- *If you don't have the number with you, make sure you keep your boarding pass for the flight.* You'll need it, as well as the ticket receipt, in order to get credit.
- *Join an affinity card program.* You can significantly increase your mileage if you charge your purchase on a frequent flyer affinity card (see below).
- *Read the monthly statements for special deals.* Usually they include offers like upgrade certificates, reduced-cost car rentals and more.
- *Use mileage for upgrades, too.* The most obvious option is to redeem your airline mileage for a ticket, but many airlines also let you use mileage to upgrade to Business or First Class. On a long trip, it may be worth it, particularly in affinity clubs where you don't have a lot of mileage.

Join a Travel Affinity Card Program

Many airlines, hotel chains, and charge card companies themselves sponsor charge cards that earn you mileage or lodging credits in various frequent flyer/stayer programs. It's a particularly good deal if you use one to purchase airfare or lodging, because you actually get double credit: once for the air travel or hotel stay, and once on the purchase amount.

For application information call:

Airline-Sponsored Programs

Alaska Airlines (MC, V, MC Gold)	1-800-552-7302
America West Airlines (V)	1-800-243-7762
American Airlines/Citibank (MC, V)	1-800-359-4444
Continental Airlines (MC, V, MC Gold, V Gold)	1-800-446-5336
Northwest Airlines (V, V Gold)	1-800-945-2004
TWA (V)	1-800-445-1336
United Airlines (V, MC Gold, V Gold)	1-800-537-7783
(in Illinois only)	1-708-931-1450
USAir (V, V Gold)	1-800-759-6262

Lodging-Sponsored Programs

Best Western (MC)	1-800-668-0276
(For V, V Gold)	1-800-847-7378
Kampgrounds of America	1-800-247-8101
Ramada Inns (MC, MC Gold)	1-800-672-6232

Charge Card-Sponsored Programs

American Express Membership Miles	1-800-274-6453
Citicorp Diners Club	1-800-525-9135

These suggestions we've outlined above are things you can do to help you get the most from your travel dollars without doing anything out of the ordinary. On the next pages, we discuss four other options that may work for you:

1. *Cut-rate commission-rebate agencies* that ticket you for a flat fee and return a portion of their commission to you.
2. *Consolidators,* who often get great deals on airfare, lodgings, and more.
3. *Barter programs* that allow you to exchange your products/services for travel credits.
4. *Hotel programs and reservations networks* that obtain discounts for their users.

These options are absolutely legal, often flexible enough to accommodate even the craziest travel schedules, and can save you a significant amount of money.

Cut-Rate Agencies/Commission-Rebaters

Cut-rate agencies will charge you a flat fee for making airline reservations, hotel accommodations, and more, and in turn rebate about half (sometimes a little more) of their commission. Result: Your ticket costs you a minimum of 4–7% less than the "list" price, plus the fee. In addition, because these are high volume agencies, they also often get deeply discounted fares from cruise and tour operators and some airlines—so the combined savings of discount and rebate can be considerable.

Some caveats: When doing your break-even calculations, remember that the commission rebate is calculated based on the pretax cost of the ticket, not the total ticket price. Also, these agencies are "no frills"—you have to do the homework and tell them what flight, hotel, etc. you want to book. They don't provide trip planning, advice or hand-holding. And unlike a full-service agency, they won't do the research to ensure you've found the lowest fare or contact you if fares drop between the time you book and the time you leave.

When does using a rebating agency make sense?

- When you're buying a high-priced ticket.
- When you're buying a travel service that you know is never discounted.
- When you know you have located the lowest fare available.
- When the price is not likely to change before your trip—or you're willing to keep monitoring the price yourself.

We've listed the three major U.S. rebaters on the next pages. But bear in mind that there are a number of other ways to obtain rebates:

- Check your Visa or MasterCard statements. Many banks offer travel-agency services, working through companies called credit-card enhancers. Services, fees, and procedures are similar to the independent fee-rebating agencies we've included here.
- Join a Travel Club (see below). Many offer a fee-rebate service.
- Ask your full-service travel agent if he or she will rebate part of the

commission, particularly on trips where you've done all the research yourself and all they have to do is book. You won't get the same deep rebates (usually, they'll agree to well under 5%), but it never hurts to ask.

Consolidators and Discounters

Also known as "bucket shops," consolidators have contracts with major airlines to purchase their unsold seats at major discounts (some have arrangements with hotel, cruise and tour operators, too). They then resell these tickets directly to the public, or to other travel agencies ("discounters") who sell them to the public at a steeply discounted price. (Note: Even some full-service agencies offer discounted tickets. Be sure to ask!)

Consolidators can give you big discounts on trips where you can't purchase two weeks in advance, stay over a Saturday night, or are only going one way. Discounts on domestic fares can exceed 50% off the advertised unrestricted Economy rates, and on international flights, up to 30% off the airlines' cheapest Economy excursion fares (especially during high-traffic summer months—savings are less during off-season). Business and First Class discounts are lower, around 20%, but still can provide a major saving to business travelers.

If they're offering such terrific discounts, why doesn't everyone use them? First, a lot of people don't know about them—they're fairly low profile and don't advertise extensively. Second, they're definitely no-frills —a clear case of "getting what you pay for." They usually won't deliver, sometimes they are hard to get through to on the phone, and some either won't take a credit card or they'll add the credit card commission to the price. Third, a lot of people are leery about using them because they have a reputation for sleaziness. Consolidators are unregulated, and it's true that some are financially unsound or downright crooked. To avoid scams:

- Make sure they're selling you a ticket on a regularly scheduled flight, not a charter. Charters are typically more crowded, less reliable, and absolutely hellish at check-in time.
- Beware of agencies that advertise very high (50–70%) discounts off Business and First Class prices. Chances are they're selling award coupons purchased from frequent fliers—a practice that violates airline rules, and could leave you with an unusable ticket.

- *Always* pay by credit card (this allows you to dispute the charge if something goes wrong).
- Check with the airline on which you're ticketed to make sure you have a reservation, and you're flying a regularly scheduled commercial flight, not a charter.

The final drawback is a big one: You have very little flexibility. Tickets are good only on issuing airline and only for the flight for which they were issued. Although you can specify the date, you often don't have as much say in the airline, flight time or route. The flights usually do not qualify for frequent flyer points, there may be substantial penalties for cancellation or missed flights, and you can't upgrade your ticket.

Still game? Read on. There are hundreds of consolidators/discounters throughout the U.S. We've selected for inclusion here those who accept credit cards, provide tickets for North American destinations (as well as other worldwide areas) and issue Business and First Class tickets.

You can locate other consolidators by:

- Checking the small-print ads listing low fares to various destinations in the Sunday travel section of your local newspaper.
- Checking *Consumer Reports Travel Letter* or *Consumer Reports 1993 Travel Buying Guide,* pp. 28–37.

The chart on page 228 summarizes the services of the consolidators we've included.

Barter Programs

Many airlines, hotels, car rental agencies and restaurants issue barter credits to their suppliers. This allows them to receive the goods and services they need while using their excess capacity and conserving cash. Suppliers can use the credits themselves, or trade them with other firms or intermediaries ("barter exchanges").

If you have barter-able goods and services, you could join a barter exchange typically paying an enrollment fee of up to $600 and a yearly fee of $100. As other members of the exchange use your goods, you earn credit that you can use on travel purchases (or, for that matter, any goods or services available through the exchange). You "sell" your goods at their normal selling price, and "purchase" bartered goods at their normal selling

Summary of Consolidator Services

Agency	Africa	Asia	Carib.	Europe	Hawaii	N. Am.	S. Am.	S. Pac.?	Srchge
Aereo Travel	•	•	•	•	•	•	•	•	Yes
Asia Travel Svc		•				•			No
Australia/NZ Travel		•	•	•	•	•	•		Yes
BritishEuropean Travel		•	•	•	•	•	•	•	Yes
Canatours		•		•		•			No
Carefree Getaway		•	•	•	•	•	•	•	Yes
Cheap Tickets		•		•	•	•		•	Yes
Community Travel Svc.		•	•	•	•	•	•	•	Yes
Compare Travel		•		•		•	•	•	Yes
Custom Travel		•	•	•		•		•	Yes

Agency	Africa	Asia	Carib.	Europe	Hawaii	N. Am.	S. Am.	S. Pac.?	Srchge
EZ Travel*		•		•		•	•	•	Yes
Fare Deals	•	•	•	•	•	•	•	•	Yes
Globe Travel		•		•	•	•		•	Yes
New Wave		•	•	•	•	•	•	•	Yes
Omniglobe		•		•	•	•		•	Yes
Pennsylvania Travel		•		•		•		•	Yes
Riverside		•		•	•	•	•	•	No
Skytours				•		•	•	•	Yes
Travel Avenue		•		•		•	•	•	No
Vacances Escomptes		•	•	•		•	•	•	No

*Also is a major supplier of tickets to the Middle East

price. Note: You have to declare bartered "sales" as income—but you can deduct "purchases."

For information on the barter exchange nearest you, send a self-addressed, stamped envelope to the International Reciprocal Trade Association ("IRTA"), 9513 Beach Mill Road, Great Fall, VA 22066.

Discounted Hotel Programs

There are a number of discount hotel programs that offer additional ways to save while traveling:

- *Hotel-commissioned reservation networks* are commissioned by hotels in selected cities. They will get you at least the lowest corporate rate— and in many cases, an additional 10–20% off. You don't have to join anything or pay any membership fees. The bad news is that they're not available in every city. The good news is that the sources we're providing cover major cities in North America and Europe.
- *Half-price hotel programs* provide discounts of 50%, year round, off the "published" rate at thousands of U.S. hotels—budget, deluxe, chains, independents, resorts and business hotels. The cost is low compared to the potential savings—typically, $20–100 per year. Therefore, belonging to a half-price program should be a key part of your money-saving travel strategies. The programs are simple to use: You join, the organization mails you a membership card and a directory that lists all the hotels in the program, and when you're ready to travel, you call and make a reservation. It can really be a good deal. But bear in mind a couple of things:
  - There will be times when you can't get the discount, as rooms are rented only "subject to availability"—typically, when they expect lower than 80% occupancy. Sometimes, you may have to settle for a smaller discount, or even pay rack rate.
- Some unscrupulous operators publish an inflated rate, so that the "50% discount off the published rate" isn't really half of what you'd be quoted at the desk. If you're suspicious, call them again without mentioning the 50% program and see what rate they quote.
- You usually can't just walk in and get the 50% discount; you have to call the hotel and make a booking before arriving. And you'll have to show that you really belong to the program to get the discount; don't forget to bring program I.D.

- You'll probably have to make the bookings yourself unless you have a particularly accommodating travel agent; these rates are not commissionable.

By now, you should be convinced that there are myriad ways to cut down on the high cost of travel, even if you can't always take advantage of leisure fares and other tourist-related programs. The sources listed on the next pages can help you do so.

SOURCES:

TRAVEL

AEREO TRAVEL
731 Market Street, Suite 401
San Francisco, CA 94103

1-800-755-8747
1-415-989-8747

**Type of Travel
Service:**   Consolidator.

Product Line: Provides discounted tickets to Africa, Asia,
Caribbean, Europe, Hawaii, North America,
South America and South Pacific. Also offers
charters, cruises, hotels, tours at up to 30% off.

Fax: 1-415-247-8737

Information: Phone, in office (limited assistance—know what
you want before you call).

**Orders Accepted
By:**   Phone, fax.

Payment: Cash, checks, American Express, Visa, MasterCard,
Discover. Surcharge on credit cards.

AMERICA AT 50% DISCOUNT
c/o Taste Publications
1031 Crumble Bridge Road
Baltimore, MD 21286

1-800-248-2783
1-410-825-3463

America at 50% Discount offers savings at a broad range of hotels—approximately 1000 throughout the U.S., including Alaska and Hawaii. It also offers a range of discounts on other goods and services; see below. Tip: The normal annual fee for this program is $49.95—but the customer service representative told us if you mentioned you'd seen this offer in "Money" magazine, the price drops to $19.95.

Type of Travel Service: Half-Price Hotel Program.

Product Line: Half-price hotel program; chain discounts at Stouffers (up to 25%), and Super ★8 and Travelodge (10%), restaurant discounts (typically, 25%) at some hotels, cruise and condo discounts, discounted movie tickets by mail for participating AMC, General Cinema, Loews and UA theaters.

Fax: 1-410-825-1002

Information: Phone.

Orders Accepted By: Phone, mail.

Payment: Visa, MasterCard, check or money order. Annual fee: $49.95; however, if you mention *Money* magazine, will honor $19.95 offer.

ASIA TRAVEL SERVICE
2250 Kalakaua Avenue, #506
Honolulu, HI 96815

1-800-926-0550

Type of Travel Service: Consolidator.

Product Line: Offers highly discounted airfare tickets to Asia and North America. Also offers discounted cruises, hotels, tours.

Fax: 1-808-924-2177

Information: Phone, in office (limited assistance—know what you want before you call).

Orders Accepted
By: Phone, fax.

Payment: Cash, checks, MasterCard, Visa, with no
                            surcharge.

AUSTRALIA/NEW ZEALAND (ANZ) TRAVEL
25301 Cabot Road
Laguna Hills, CA 92653

1-800-735-3861
1-800-281-4449 (in California)
1-714-586-1112

Type of Travel
Service: Consolidator.

Product Line: Offers highly discounted airfare tickets to Asia and
                            North America. Also offers discounted cruises,
                            hotels, tours.

Fax: 1-714-586-1124

Information: Phone, in office (limited assistance—know what
                            you want before you call).

Orders Accepted
By: Phone, fax.

Payment: Cash, checks, American Express, Discover,
                            MasterCard, Visa. Surcharge on credit cards.

BET TRAVEL
841 Blossom Hill Road, Suite 212C
San Jose, CA 95123

1-800-747-1476
1-408-229-7880

Type of Travel
Service: Consolidator.

Product Line: Provides consolidator-discounted tickets to Asia,
                            Caribbean, Europe, Hawaii, North America,
                            South America, South Pacific. Also offers charters.

Fax:	1-408-365-1101
Information:	Phone, in office (limited assistance—know what you want before you call).
Orders Accepted By:	Phone, fax.
Payment:	Cash, checks, American Express, MasterCard, Visa. Surcharge on credit cards.

CANATOURS
427 Bernard Street
Los Angeles, CA 90012

1-213-223-1111

Type of Travel Service:	Consolidator.
Product Line:	Provides highly discounted tickets to Asia, Europe and North America. Also offers cruises, hotels and tours.
Fax:	1-213-223-1048
Information:	Phone, in office (limited assistance—know what you want before you call).
Orders Accepted By:	Phone, fax.
Payment:	Cash, checks, American Express, MasterCard, Visa. No surcharge on credit cards.

CAREFREE GETAWAY TRAVEL
701 N. Walnut Street
Roanoke, TX 76262

1-800-969-8687
1-817-430-1128

Type of Travel Service:	Consolidator.

Product Line: Provides highly discounted tickets to Asia, Europe and North America. Also offers cruises, hotels and tours.

Fax: 1–817–430–0522

Information: Phone, in office (limited assistance—know what you want before you call).

Orders Accepted By: Phone, fax.

Payment: Cash, check, American Express, MasterCard, Visa, Discover. Surcharge on credit cards.

CHEAP TICKETS
1695 Kapiolani Blvd.
Honolulu, HI 96814

1–800–234–4522
1–800–377–1000
1–808–947–3717
Overland Park, KS (phone orders only):
1–800–234–4522
1–800–377–1000
1–913–384–1404

Type of Travel Service: Consolidator.

Product Line: Offers discounted tickets to Asia, Europe, Hawaii, North America, and South Pacific. Also offers charters and hotels.

Fax: National: 1–800–284–4443
Honolulu only: 1–808–946–5993

Information: Phone, in office (limited assistance—know what you want before you call).

Orders Accepted By: Phone, fax.

Payment: Cash, check, American Express, MasterCard, Visa. Surcharge on credit cards.

COMMUNITY TRAVEL SERVICE
5299 College Avenue
Oakland, CA 94618

1-510-653-0990

Type of Travel Service:	Consolidator.
Product Line:	Provides discounted tickets to Asia, Caribbean, Europe, Hawaii, North America, South America and South Pacific. Also offers charters, cruises, hotels and tours.
Fax:	1-510-653-9071
Information:	Phone, in office (limited assistance—know what you want before you call).
Orders Accepted By:	Phone, fax.
Payment:	Cash, check, American Express, MasterCard, Visa. No surcharge on credit cards.

COMPARE TRAVEL
5 North Wabash Avenue, Suite 818
Chicago, IL 60602

1-312-853-1144

Type of Travel Service:	Consolidator.
Product Line:	Offers consolidator-discounted airfare to Asia, Europe, Hawaii, North America, South America and South Pacific. Also offers cruises, hotels and tours.
Fax:	1-312-853-2446
Information:	Phone, in office (limited assistance—know what you want before you call).

**Orders Accepted
By:** Phone, fax.

Payment: Cash, check, MasterCard, Visa. Surcharge on
credit cards.

CUSTOM TRAVEL
6145 Mission Street
Daly City, CA 94014

1-800-535-9797
1-415-239-4200

**Type of Travel
Service:** Consolidator.

Product Line: Provides discounted airfare tickets to Asia,
Caribbean, Europe, Hawaii, North America,
South America and South Pacific. Also offers
charters and tours.

Fax: 1-415-239-0121

Information: Phone, in office (limited assistance—know what
you want before you call).

**Orders Accepted
By:** Phone, fax.

Payment: Cash, check, MasterCard, Visa. Surcharge on
credit cards.

ENTERTAINMENT PUBLICATIONS
2125 Butterfield Road
Troy, MI 48084

1-800-477-3234
1-313-637-8400

It's easy to become a member of Entertainment Publication's half-price
club: All you do is purchase one of their directories. The directories will
give you the names and telephone numbers of the thousands of hotels,
restaurants, etc. that participate in this program. Entertainment Publications publishes 40+ directories: The best ones for business travelers are the

National Hotel Directory ($24.95 + $3 S/H) and the National Dining Directory (each, $24.95 + $3 S/H, or get both for $34.95 + $3 S/H). A tip: If you travel extensively to one city, you might purchase an individual city directory, which will provide discounts on a broad selection of local restaurants, as well as some limited hotel discounts. They offer books for many U.S. cities, plus some directories for European cities, including London, Amsterdam, Stockholm and more.

Type of Travel Service:	Half-price hotel program.
Product Line:	50% off published rack rates at 3500+ U.S. hotels; 10% discounts at most locations of Choice Hotels, Doubletree, Howard Johnson, Residence Inn by Marriott and TraveLodge; discount coupons for restaurants, usually 25% off or second entree free; $25–100 discounts off Continental Airline fares, depending on ticket price; discounts off automotive services, car rentals, and visitor attractions (usually, 2-for-1).
Fax:	N/A.
Information:	Phone.
Orders Accepted By:	Phone for directories. To make a reservation at a hotel, call the hotel directly, using the number in the directory.
Payment:	MasterCard, Visa, check or money order for purchase of directory. Payment at individual hotels is subject to their particular credit policies.

EXPRESS RESERVATIONS

3800 Arapahoe Road
Boulder, CO 80303

1-800-356-1123
1-303-440-8481

Express Reservations only operates in New York and Los Angeles—but at savings of 10–30% off published rates, it's worth remembering when you visit these cities. Most of the time, they'll beat the corporate rate. And they have arrangements with many different levels of hotels, so you can find something that fits your budget.

**Type of Travel
Service:**   Hotel-commissioned reservation network.

Product Line: Discounts (10–30% off published rates) on wide
                         range of hotels (per night rates range from under
                         $100 to $225) in Los Angeles and New York. Last
                         room availability—even if there's only one room
                         left at the hotel, you can get it at the discounted
                         rate.

Fax: 1–303–440–0166

Information: Phone.

**Orders Accepted
By:**   Phone, fax.

Payment: You pay the hotel directly. There is no fee for
                        their service.

EZ TRAVEL
4759 Brooklyn Avenue N.E.
Northwest Suite
Seattle, WA 98105

1–206–524–1977

**Type of Travel
Service:**   Consolidator.

Product Line: Offers consolidator airfares to Asia, Europe,
                         Middle East, North America, South America and
                         South Pacific. Also offers charters, hotels, tours.
                         Specializes in Europe and Middle East discount
                         airfares.

Fax: 1–206–524–1982

Information: On phone; in office (limited assistance—know
                         what you want before you call).

Orders Accepted
By: Phone, fax.

Payment: Cash, check, American Express, MasterCard, Visa.
                             Surcharge on credit cards.

FARE DEALS TRAVEL
9350 East Arapahoe Road, Suite 330
Englewood, CO 80112

1–800–878–2929
1–303–792–2929

Type of Travel
Service: Consolidator.

Product Line: Offers consolidator airfares to Africa, Asia,
                             Caribbean, Europe, Hawaii, North America,
                             South America, South Pacific. Also offers hotel
                             deals.

Fax: 1–303–792–2954

Information: Phone, in office (limited assistance—know what
                             you want before you call).

Orders Accepted
By: Phone, fax.

Payment: Cash, check, American Express, MasterCard, Visa,
                             Discover. Surcharge on credit cards.

FARE DEALS TRAVEL
10806 Reisterstown Road, Suite 2C
Owings Mills, MD 21117

1–800–347–7006
1–410–581–8787

Type of Travel
Service: Consolidator.

Product Line: Offers consolidator airfares to Africa, Asia,
                             Caribbean, Europe, Hawaii, North America,

South America, South Pacific. Also offers hotel deals.

Fax:	1-410-581-1093
Information:	Phone, in office (limited assistance—know what you want before you call).
Orders Accepted By:	Phone, fax.
Payment:	Cash, check, MasterCard, Visa, Discover. Surcharge on credit cards.

GLOBE TRAVEL SPECIALISTS

507 Fifth Avenue, Room 606
New York, NY 10017

1-800-969-4562
1-212-682-8687

Type of Travel Service:	Consolidator.
Product Line:	Offers consolidator tickets to Asia, Europe, Hawaii, North America, South Pacific. Also offers cruises.
Fax:	1-212-682-8605
Information:	Phone, in office (limited assistance—know what you want before you call).
Orders Accepted By:	Phone, fax.
Payment:	Cash, check, MasterCard, Visa, Discover. Surcharge on credit cards.

GREAT AMERICAN TRAVELER

Access Development Corp.
P.O. Box 27563
Salt Lake City, UT 84127

1-800-548-2812

Great American Traveler has half-price arrangements with over 2100 hotels in North America and 300 hotels in Europe, and also offers condo, cruise and tour discounts through its participating travel club.

**Type of Travel
Service:** Half-price hotel program.

Product Line: Half-price hotel program, condo, cruise and tour discounts 20–50%.

Fax: 1-801-262-2311

Information: Membership includes a directory of participating hotels worldwide.

**Orders Accepted
By:** To become a member: 1-800-548-2812. Annual fee: $49.95.
To make a reservation at a hotel, call the hotel directly, using the number in the directory.

Payment: Check, money order, Visa, MasterCard, Discover and American Express. Money-back guarantee on membership: full refund within 60 days, prorated refund thereafter.

HOTEL RESERVATIONS NETWORK

8140 Walnut Hill Lane
Dallas, TX 75231

1-800-964-6835
1-214-361-7311

Hotel Reservations Network offers deep discounts off published room rates in a variety of U.S. cities, plus London and Paris. They can find you great deals: sometimes 65% off the corporate rate!

**Type of Travel
Service:** Hotel-commissioned reservation network.

Product Line: Offers deeply discounted rooms in New York, Atlanta, San Francisco, Hawaii, Washington, D.C., Boston, Chicago, Los Angeles, and New Orleans. In Europe: London and Paris.

Fax:	1–214–361–7299
Information:	Phone.
Orders Accepted By:	Phone, fax.
Payment:	You pay the hotel. There is no charge for Hotel Reservations Network's service.

NEW WAVE TRAVEL
4719 University Way NE, Suite 205
Seattle, WA 98105

1–800–220–WAVE (1–800–220–9283)
1–206–527–3579

Type of Travel Service:	Consolidator.
Product Line:	Offers consolidator tickets to Asia, Caribbean, Europe, Hawaii, North America, South America and South Pacific. Also offers cruises, hotels and tours.
Fax:	1–206–527–3241
Information:	Phone, in office (limited assistance—know what you want before you call).
Orders Accepted By:	Phone, fax.
Payment:	Cash, check, American Express, MasterCard, Visa, Discover. Surcharge on credit cards.

OMNIGLOBE TRAVEL
690 Market Street, Suite 510
San Francisco, CA 94104

1–800–894–9942
1–415–433–9312

**Type of Travel
Service:**   Consolidator.

Product Line: Offers consolidator discounts on tickets to Asia,
                          Europe, Hawaii, North America, South Pacific.
                          Also offers charters, cruises, hotels and tours.

Fax: 1-415-433-9315

Information: Phone, in office (limited assistance—know what
                          you want before you call).

**Orders Accepted
By:**   Phone, fax.

Payment: Cash, check, American Express, MasterCard, Visa.
                          Surcharge on credit cards.

PENNSYLVANIA TRAVEL

15 Maple Avenue
Paoli, PA 19301

1-800-331-0947
1-610-251-9944 (in Philadelphia area)

Pennsylvania offers both consolidator tickets and commission rebates. It
deducts the commission, up to 10%, from the cost of any itinerary for up to
four people. It then charges a flat fee, under the following structure:

Ticket Cost	Fee	Maximum Saving
$0–699	$35	$34
$700–1,499	$50	$99
$1500–3999	$100	$299

Thereafter, the fee increases $50 for each $2000 bracket.

If you pay for airfare and cruises by check, you'll pay the commission-
less amount, plus the fee. If you pay by credit card, you'll pay the whole
amount, and a rebate will be sent to you by check later. For hotels and car
rentals, you'll pay the full amount and a rebate check will be sent to you
when the commission is received by Pennsylvania.

**Type of Travel
Service:**   Commission rebater; consolidator.

Product Line: Rebates commissions, up to 10%, on airfares, hotels, cruises, and car rentals, for both domestic and international destinations. Offers consolidator airfares to Asia, Europe, North America and South Pacific. Also offers consolidator fares for charters, cruises, hotels and tours.

Fax: 1-610-644-2150

Information: Phone, in office (limited assistance—know what you want before you call).

Orders Accepted By: Phone, fax.

Payment: Cash, check, American Express, MasterCard, Visa. Surcharge on credit cards.

RIVERSIDE TRAVEL & SERVICES

1051 River Street
Honolulu, HI 96817

1-808-521-5645

Type of Travel Service: Consolidator.

Product Line: Offers consolidator deals on airfares to Asia, Europe, Hawaii, North America, South America and South Pacific. Also offers charters and tours.

Fax: 1-808-523-2342

Information: Phone, in office (limited assistance—know what you want before you call).

Orders Accepted By: Phone, fax.

Payment: Cash, check, American Express, MasterCard, Visa. No surcharge on credit cards.

SKYTOURS
26 Third Street, Suite 460
San Francisco, CA 94103

1-415-777-3544

Type of Travel Service:	Consolidator.
Product Line:	Offers consolidator airfares to Europe, North America, South America and South Pacific. Also offers charters.
Fax:	1-415-777-9290
Information:	Phone, in office (limited assistance—know what you want before you call).
Orders Accepted By:	Phone, fax.
Payment:	Cash, check, American Express, Diners Club, Discover, MasterCard, Visa. Surcharge on credit cards.

TRAVEL AVENUE
10 South Riverside Place, Suite 1404
Chicago, IL 60606

1-800-333-3335

Travel Avenue offers both consolidator tickets and commission rebates. Commissions are rebated under the following schedule (Note: There is no rebate on consolidator tickets):

- Domestic airfare: 7% rebate, versus $10 fee.
- International airfare: Average rebate is 12%, versus $25 fee.
- Cruises: Average rebate is 7%, versus $25 fee.
- Auto rental and lodging: 5%, with no fee.

For rebates, you'll pay the list price at time of purchase. In the case of air travel and cruises, you'll receive a rebate check with the tickets. For hotels and car rental, rebates are sent after travel is completed and you send the invoices to Travel Avenue.

Type of Travel Service:	Consolidator and commission rebater.
Product Line:	Offers tickets to Asia, Europe, Hawaii, North America, South America and South Pacific. Also offers charters, cruises, hotels, and tours. Also rebates portion of agent's commission. (See Commission Rebaters section of this chapter.)
Fax:	1-312-876-1254
Information:	Phone, in office (limited assistance—know what you want before you call). Note: They have a somewhat complicated voice-mail system before you get through to one of their 40 sales agents—but you can avoid it by requesting tickets or a price quote by fax.
Orders Accepted By:	Phone, fax. Tickets are sent by U.S. mail if the trip is at least 14 days off; otherwise, Fed Ex is used at an additional charge.
Payment:	Cash, check, American Express, MasterCard, Visa. No surcharge on credit cards.

THE SMART TRAVELER

3111 Southwest 27th Avenue
Miami, FL 33133

1-800-448-3338
1-305-448-3338

The Smart Traveler is a good choice if you're traveling internationally, or if you're taking a cruise. If you're traveling within the U.S. or Canada, you'd be better off using another agency, as domestic/Canadian airline tickets sold alone are not discounted. International airline tickets are discounted at a straight 4%.

For packages or travel arrangements involving multiple purchases (e.g., airline plus cruise), they offer a rebate/fee arrangement. The rebate is 10%, and is good for up to four people traveling on the same itinerary. Fees are as follows:

Ticket Cost	Fee	Maximum Saving
$0–750	$30	$35
$751–2000	$50	$200
$2001–4000	$100	$300

The fee rises $50 for each additional $2000 expenditure.

A plus: The Smart Traveler passes along to their clients any special bonuses provided to travel agents by airlines, cruise lines, and hotels, so sometimes the price is even lower than their initial quote. They also will provide brochures and other information (although they don't usually provide in-depth trip-planning services).

Another plus: There is normally no fee for changes or refunds, beyond those that the travel suppliers themselves charge.

Type of Travel Service: Consolidator and commission rebater.

Product Line: Provides rebates on international airfare, hotel, cruise and car rental commissions. The size of the rebate ranges from 4 to 10%. They also have arrangements with consolidators, charter companies and some airlines to purchase deep-discount tickets for cruises and travel abroad, and these discounts can top 50%, particularly to Asia and South America.

Fax: 1-305-443-3544

Information: Phone, in office (limited assistance—know what you want before you call). They will send brochures to aid you in your trip planning.

Orders Accepted By: Phone, fax. They will normally deliver tickets by UPS ground service. If there's a rush, they will use an overnight delivery service (additional charge if purchasing discounted tickets; otherwise, no charge).

Payment: Cash, check, American Express, MasterCard, Visa.
                      No surcharge on credit cards.

VACANCES ESCOMPTES

1255 Phillips Square, Suite 1002
Montreal, Quebec, Canada H3B 3G1

1-514-861-9090

**Type of Travel
Service:**   Consolidator.

Product Line: Offers tickets to Asia, Caribbean, Europe, North
                       America, South America and South Pacific. Also
                       offers charters, cruises, hotels and tours.

Fax: Not available.

Information: Phone, in office (limited assistance—know what
                       you want before you call).

**Orders Accepted
By:**   Phone, fax.

Payment: Cash, check, American Express, MasterCard, Visa.
                       No surcharge on credit cards.

Index

PRODUCTS